Practical Zen

for Health, Wealth and Mindfulness

Julian Daizan Skinner with Sarah Bladen

Foreword by Shinzan Miyamae

SINGING
DRAGON

LONDON AND PHILADELPHIA

Caution: The practices and techniques described herein are not to be used as an alternative to professional medical treatment. This presentation does not attempt to give any medical diagnosis, treatment, prescription or suggestion for medication in relation to any human disease or physical condition.

This material is intended to supplement individual instruction by a competent teacher. Anyone who undertakes these practices on the basis of this material alone does so entirely at his or her own risk.

Zenways is not and cannot be held responsible for the consequences of any practice or misuse of the information presented here. Consult with your doctor before embarking on any meditation or exercise programme.

First published in 2018
by Singing Dragon
an imprint of Jessica Kingsley Publishers
73 Collier Street
London N1 9BE, UK
and
400 Market Street, Suite 400
Philadelphia, PA 19106, USA

www.singingdragon.com

Library of Congress Cataloging in Publication Data
Names: Skinner, Julian Daizan, 1963- author.
Title: Practical Zen for health, wealth, and mindfulness / Julian Daizan
    Skinner, with Sarah Bladen ; foreword by Shinzan Miyamae.
Description: Philadelphia : Jessica Kingsley Publishers, 2018.
Identifiers: LCCN 2017050305 | ISBN 9781848193901
Subjects: LCSH: Meditation--Zen Buddhism. | Well-being.
Classification: LCC BQ9289.5 .S625 2018 | DDC 294.3/4435--dc23 LC record available
at https://lccn.loc.gov/2017050305

British Library Cataloguing in Publication Data
A CIP catalogue record for this book is available from the British Library

ISBN 978 1 84819 390 1
eISBN 978 0 85701 347 7

Printed and bound in Great Britain

'People sometimes think of Zen as a little ethereal and not something they can easily apply to their lives. This book entirely dispels such myths. It is a grounded, practical guide to how Zen can make a profound difference to your life in the here and now. I, like many around the world today, can personally attest to this, and indeed to Daizan's unique ability to teach and convey it. His clarity of voice, wisdom and dedication to the welfare of others shines clearly through the whole book, and I have no doubt that it will make a lasting impact on all who are fortunate enough to read it.'
– *Professor Russell Razzaque, psychiatrist and writer*

'We all want to be the best version of who we are, but not many of us get to be that. If by some chance you do get there, it's fleeting, giving a glimpse of what we can achieve, then the focus disappears. But it doesn't have to be that way. Daizan is the most amazing example of a human being who has found the best version of himself that I have ever encountered...but make no mistake, it didn't happen by accident, he worked at it. My meeting with him was no accident, and neither is the fact that you have picked up this book and are reading these words. This book will help you become who you really were supposed to be, and ARE!'
– *Joe Pasquale, comedian*

'As always, Daizan writes with clarity and assurance and from a place of huge compassion. The contents of this book are the foundations upon which all of the teaching at Serenity Retreat happens. I'm pretty sure it's the groundedness of the teachings that ensures that people keep coming back! This book is accessible, kind and real. I particularly liked the section on wealth which can often be a very confusing subject for spiritual seekers. I would strongly recommend it to anyone who is looking to start a meditation practice or anyone who is confused about what meditation is all about, or how it can be.'
– *Kim Bennett, entrepreneur and founder of Serenity Retreat*

by the same author

Practical Zen
Meditation and Beyond
Julian Daizan Skinner
Foreword by Shinzan Miyamae
ISBN 978 1 84819 363 5
eISBN 978 0 85701 321 7

Contents

Foreword

Zen has many dimensions. The Japanese Rinzai school in which I trained has a strong emphasis on wellbeing arising out of the ill health and recovery of the great Zen master Hakuin Ekaku (1686–1769). This tradition has had a lasting influence on Japanese society, continuing until today.

Influenced by Hakuin and also by the great Zen populariser Bankei Yōtaku (1622–1693), founder of Gyokuryuji temple, my teaching seat, I have sought to cast the net as widely as possible and make the benefits of Zen practice available to everyone – those interested in being strong and healthy as well as those with existential concerns.

This has brought me close to condemned murderers, mafia members, those who have rejected society (*hikikomori*[1]), as well as many in the mainstream population. Successful people have also come to me to seek ways to develop greater happiness and further success.

---

1   In Japanese, meaning 'reclusive adults or adolescents who withdraw from social life, often seeking extreme degrees of isolation and confinement'.

Underlying the work of Zen is the conviction that human beings can change. The teachings never promise that change is easy, but they do maintain it is possible. The key term in bringing about this change is found in the Japanese word *shugyo*, which we can translate as 'systematic practice'.

You have in your hands a manual of systematic Zen practice, which, if followed, will bring about tremendous positive change in your life. Written by my successor Daizan, together with journalist and Zen practitioner Sarah Bladen, this book gives you everything you need to create the all-important foundation through which positive transformation can flourish.

I have seen the results of Daizan's teaching activities with my own eyes, both in Japan and on my visits to the West. Over many years he has wholeheartedly dedicated himself to absorbing the tradition while at the same time being aware of the needs of modern society. Daizan has successfully strengthened rather than watered down the effectiveness of this work. For instance, I am delighted with his adaptation of Hakuin's *nanso no ho* (healing ointment meditation) in Chapters 1 and 2 of this text, which is simple, practical and particularly effective in today's troubled world.

We live in a time in which our delicate planet is too small for closed-hearted, unconscious ways of living. Each year the devastation spreads. Despite fortunes spent on space programmes, we have found nowhere else in the universe where human beings can flourish. Thus we have no choice but to change, and the location of this sustainable change must begin in the human heart.

This Zen cultivation of health, wellbeing and optimal function is surely a force for the good of the individual, for society and for the world. Please work earnestly with these methods. Wishing you many benefits from your practice.

Shinzan Miyamae,
Gyokuryuji, Gifu, Japan

Preface

Sarah on Daizan

Growing up, I had many existential questions and a burning thirst for answers. Then, in 2012, I lost my dad to cancer, broke up with my boyfriend and my dream job disappeared, all within the same month. These losses were heart-breaking at the time but turned out to be great awakeners for me, guiding me to finally go on an inward journey. As the Zen proverb goes, 'No mud, no lotus.' And that's when I immersed myself in meditation and mindfulness.

When I first came across my Zen mentor, Julian Daizan Skinner, he emanated a radiant calmness, a dynamic sense of Zen, something otherworldly. In 2007 he had been named his teacher's successor and had returned to the UK with nothing. By the time I met him he was already London's leading Zen teacher. I knew instantly that he was a genuine master, someone I could trust and learn so much from. I believe our meeting was no coincidence; rather, it was synchronistic, as it happened at exactly the right time in my life. Daizan has an innate knowingness and a very practical way of bringing Zen to the modern world, so it is relevant and meaningful. It felt natural to enrol on his Zen teacher training courses to deepen my practice.

After spending more time with Daizan, it was evident that he lives in the present moment, has much compassion for others and lives his life with great freedom and inner contentment.

To me, Zen makes so much sense, especially in today's fast-paced, often stressful world. Once I began grasping the mindfulness tools, a powerful transformation took place.

When I first began practice, it wasn't easy – my mind raced, but with practice, I learned to dis-identify from my thoughts, and over time, my doubts and anxiety slowly dissolved too. It was incredibly liberating when I could finally sit down and experience a blissful, silent meditation. Now, I look forward to daily practice. When I sit in stillness and connect to my breath, I immediately experience a sense of calmness, even if events around me are chaotic.

Along with yoga and dance, Zen meditation and mindfulness have helped me maintain a strong immune system and high energy levels. When uncertainty or unexpected events arise, the practice has given me a doorway to clarity. One of the great miracles of practising Zen is that I no longer feel a nagging void or a sense of separation with the world. And if a change of this magnitude can happen to me, it can happen to anyone.

Daizan on Sarah

I first met Sarah when she came on a Zenways meditation and mindfulness teacher training programme. At the time she was a journalist with strong Middle East connections. She'd spent considerable time in the war-torn rubble of Beirut and had edited the popular *OK!* magazine in Dubai. Here was somebody at home in and able to connect with vastly different worlds. Combined with her clear and obvious thirst for the work, her innate and developed communication abilities made her a natural to join forces with when it came time to write this book. She has the speed of a professional, which has brought my own pedestrian rate of production into sharp focus. It's been a delight to see her work with this material and bring it to new audiences in Israel, India and also now back in the UK. Thank you, Sarah.

Acknowledgements

I don't find book writing easy. In climbing this particular mountain, I'm grateful to have had Sarah Bladen as a fellow alpiniste. She has been consistently positive in her attitude and rapid in her production. Thank you, Sarah, for bringing such good humour and grace to the process.

My teachers, Zen masters Shinzan and Daishin, continue to inspire and inform my work. My sense of Zen practice and its potentials flows primarily from their Zen practice and their selfless sharing of its fruits. Both teachers have displayed significant concern over how this work can be transplanted into Western soil. Both of them have taught me much about the health and wellbeing dimensions of Zen practice.

Over the past decade of sharing this work in the Western world, my own practice has continued to evolve through and alongside many fellow travellers. Vital to this book has been the Zenways team of teacher trainers who have been actively involved in both the development and dissemination of these practices. Mark Kuren Wesmoquette, Kim Bennett, Matt Shinkai Kane, Sean Rinryu Collins and Melanie Hoetsu Shinton have all contributed beyond measure. In addition I'd like to thank the more than 50 Zenways meditation and mindfulness teachers around the world who share these processes and practices, and are creating an ever-widening sphere of living connection with the work.

Thank you to the Zen meditation and mindfulness practitioners who have been willing to tell their stories for the book.

I'd like to thank Dr Barbara Jikai Gabrys and Professor Maryanne Martin for their University of Oxford research project studying the outcomes from these practices, which continues to develop interesting insights.

Author, spiritual teacher and dear friend Jonathan Harrison has been selflessly generous in making sure this work finds the right publisher.

Samantha Warrington has selflessly and skilfully done wonders with the raw (and very rough) manuscript.

I want to mention again Matt Shinkai Kane who has been closely involved in this book at many stages, particularly with background research.

Thank you to Meijia Ling, Pali translator extraordinaire.

Special thanks to psychiatrist Dr Russell Razzaque, who is deeply involved in sharing Zen meditation and mindfulness and the transformatively powerful mindfulness-supported mental health treatment 'Open Dialogue' in the UK health service. It was Russell who gently suggested that the time might be right for a book like this.

Thank you to the experts on mindfulness of money, Scott Brown, Lynn Exley, Frank Cooke and Joanna Bodimeade.

Thank you so much to Jessica Kingsley and the staff at Singing Dragon. It has been a delight to work with Emily Badger, Sophie Raoufi, Victoria Peters and the team.

Lastly, and always, I wish to thank my parents, Kevin and Judy.

Establishing Your Baseline

I've been teaching meditation for many years. I can't tell you the number of times I've had people come to me feeling pretty miserable. Over a few weeks' practice I've noticed them brighten up, even massively transform. However, at that point, on asking them how life's going, they frequently reply something like, 'I think it might be working. I'm not sure.' They simply can't remember how miserable they were, even a few weeks previously. This extraordinary human adaptability is mostly a blessing, but in this situation it works against the motivation to continue practising. I began searching around for some objective measures that would show people what they'd achieved. Dr Barbara Jikai Gabrys, Zen master and University of Oxford teacher, helped me enormously. She organised for us a battery of psychological tests. This led on to an Oxford research project on the Zenways practices you'll find in this book, led by Professor Maryanne Martin and still ongoing. You can self-administer three of these tests, before and after following the practices in this book.

We have three scales available for you. Let's have a look at them.

With a long track record of use (initially published in 1983), the *Perceived Stress Scale* (PSS) gives you a value related to how you're feeling about the stress dimension of your life. Dr Sheldon Cohen, the Scale developer, writes: 'It is a measure of the degree to which situations in one's life are appraised as stressful. Items were designed to tap how unpredictable, uncontrollable, and overloaded respondents find their lives.'[1]

Published by Professor Ed Diener *et al.* in 1985,[2] the *Satisfaction With Life Scale* (SWLS) only takes a minute or so to complete and gives a rating of how you feel about the totality of your life. Satisfaction with life is an essential component of happiness.

The *Mindful Attention Awareness Scale* (MAAS)[3] is designed to measure the 'receptive state of mind in which attention, informed by a sensitive awareness of what is occurring in the present, simply observes what is taking place'. Developed by Drs Kirk Warren Brown and Richard M. Ryan, at the University of Rochester, New York, and published in 2003, the MAAS takes only five minutes or so to complete.

So, I suggest, go to the website associated with this book[4] and complete the scales right now. It'll only take a few minutes. Then, when you're ready to begin these practices (whether it's a few hours or, even better, a few days later), revisit the website

---

1   Cohen, S. (1994) *Perceived Stress Scale.* Menlo Park, CA: Mind Garden, Inc. Available at www.mindgarden.com/documents/PerceivedStressScale.pdf

2   Diener, E., Emmons, R.A., Larsen, R.J. and Griffin, S. (1985) 'The Satisfaction With Life Scale.' *Journal of Personality Assessment 49*, 1, 71.

3   Brown, K.W. and Ryan, R.M. (2003) 'The benefits of being present: Mindfulness and its role in psychological wellbeing.' *Journal of Personality and Social Psychology 84*, 822–848. See also https://ggsc.berkeley.edu/images/uploads/The_Mindful_Attention_Awareness_Scale_-_State.pdf

4   Go to www.zenways.org/practical-zen-health-survey

and complete the scales again. From this point you'll be able to access the guided meditation recordings on the website.

Once you've completed the course of practices given in the book, come back a third time to the website and complete the scales again. You'll receive an email showing you how these indices have changed for you over the period you've been practising, and access to interpretation materials.

CHAPTER 1

Setting the Scene

'Just as physical exercise is good in a general way for the body, so zazen (meditation) on this level is undoubtedly beneficial to both physical and mental health.'[1]

– Zen master Hakuun Yasutani

As we start, let's take a moment. Become aware of your right hand. What can you feel? Perhaps you are holding this book and you can feel the contact with the book; perhaps your hand can sense other things; perhaps there's a response to the air temperature. Simply bring your attention to what's here.

Now move this same attention and curiosity to your left hand. How is the experience different from your right? There's no correct or incorrect way to feel here; we're simply tuning in to what's detectable right now.

Once you've sensed your right and left hands, move your attention to the crown of your head and then downwards in a steady sweep through your body. Take perhaps ten seconds

1   Yasutani, H. (2010) 'The five kinds of Zen.' *The Middle Way: Journal of the Buddhist Society 85*, 2, August, 105.

on your journey down towards your feet. We're not trying to change anything or avoid anything; we're simply noticing what we can detect.

This very simple process, when developed, can change your life. I suspect you know this, otherwise, why read this book? And developing the quality of your attention is not difficult. It doesn't require years of study, or a high IQ or a deep level of personal development. It requires one thing and one thing only – practice. Everyone gets distracted, but if you are able to gently bring your mind back enough times, attention becomes a habit. As you foster this habit of awareness, you become able to consciously enjoy your life, you learn to let go of blocks and burdens, you might even, the science tells us, turn back the ageing clock.

What you have in your hands is a distillation of successful ways to develop the Zen meditation and mindfulness habit, taken from the tradition and developed over my own 25 years or so of practice and the practice of thousands of people who have come to me.

In putting this work into practice, you don't need to believe anything. In fact, I strongly recommend you keep your wits about you. Look out for my blind spots – even though I can't see them, I know they're there. Nevertheless, I'm pretty sure I can be of help to you. This material is pretty heavily road-tested. You're not alone; we can do this together. Together, let's change your life.

Almost every week people come to Yugagyo Dojo, my practice centre in London, wanting to learn to meditate. The Japanese word *Zen* means meditation, and I've spent most of my adult life studying and practising the Zen forms of inner development. When new students arrive, I always begin by asking about their intentions.

'Some people come here,' I tell them, 'because they want to solve a problem – they want to sleep better, or to access their creativity or deal with stress, even make more money or be happier in their relationships.'

'All these,' I continue, 'are perfectly fine aspirations. And then some people come because they want to find the place where, from the beginning, there never was a problem.'

This book is for the first type of people. For the second group, those interested in awakening to a wholly new reality, there is a companion volume to this one, called *Practical Zen*.[2]

My own teacher welcomed people this way. Regardless of their motivations, everyone was equally welcome. It was a common sight in his temple to have a homeless person sitting in meditation beside a member of the Bridgestone manufacturing dynasty (the largest tyre manufacturers in the world), next to a schoolboy, next to a ten-year monk, each one with different intentions.

This distinction of motivations for Zen practice is not new. It goes back over a thousand years to a Zen master in the 8th century called Keiho Shumitsu. He actually further subdivided the motivations for practice into five, but the distinctions we highlight above capture the main elements of his wisdom.[3]

To introduce a couple of Japanese terms, those with a problem-solving motivation are considered to be practising what is called *bompu Zen*. The character *bon* (it shifts to *bom* in combination) means 'ordinary', 'worldly' or 'common'. *Pu* is

2   Skinner, J.D. (2017) *Practical Zen: Meditation and Beyond*. London: Singing Dragon.

3   An excellent and detailed exposition of the five types of practice by Ven. Anzan Hoshin Roshi may be found at https://wwzc.org/dharma-text/begin-here-five-styles-zen

the character for 'man'.[4] You could translate it as mundane or secular Zen. By contrast, the other type of intention leads to *satori Zen* – 'waking-up Zen'.[5]

Twentieth-century Japanese Zen master Hakuun Yasutani described *bompu Zen* like this:

> It is *zazen* (sitting meditation) practised simply and solely for the sake of improving physical and mental health. It has nothing to do with either religion or philosophy... My teacher used to say that he would like to see everybody without exception practising this kind of Zen. For just as physical exercise is good for the body, so *zazen* on this level is undoubtedly beneficial to both physical and mental health.[6]

I want to introduce you to my first meditation teacher, Catholic priest Father Jack Madden, a family friend when I was growing up in Kent.

In my teens I remember him coming quite regularly to supper. A tall, broad-shouldered Irishman, he was, like my father, a natural sportsman. They shared a commitment to golf. Father Jack wasn't just keen on golf; he was passionate about it.

Sitting around the supper table one evening, he revealed his secret weapon. 'Meditation. I spend 20 minutes every day doing meditation, and my game's gone through the roof!'

I had no interest in golf, but I was intrigued. I was already vaguely aware of the image of meditating Himalayan yogis and similar stereotypes. But this was different. This was something

---

4 凡夫禅: *Bompu Zen*, regular person's meditation.

5 悟り禅: *Satori Zen*, meditation for awakening.

6 Yasutani, H. (2010) 'The five kinds of Zen.' *The Middle Way: Journal of the Buddhist Society* 85, 2, August, 105.

practical, non-spiritual, simply another dimension of his golf training programme. I asked Father Jack to teach me, and he did. He directed me to sit comfortably and put my attention on to an Indian sacred word. 'Every time you drift off,' he said, 'just bring your mind back to it.' It sounded so simple. From then on, I, too, put in my 20 minutes a day. Initially there was far more drifting than attention. Sometimes I seemed to spend the whole 20 minutes floating in space. Now and again I remembered to re-focus. I was amazed at what a butterfly mind I had! For the first month or two, I doubted whether I could keep the syllable in my attention for more than a minute or two. I got pretty discouraged, convinced that I was never going to be any good at this meditation business, but even the distraction was pleasant, so I carried on.

Father Jack wasn't alone in being a golf-loving clergyman. Catholic priests have a well-established and very competitive golf league. He went on to become an all-England priest champion.

In the years since, vast numbers of sports people have taken to the 'inner game'. Father Jack was an early adopter. I spoke to him recently, almost 40 years on, as he prepared for retirement from the parish of Beckenham in South East London. He confirmed that he still meditates every day.

Over the years I have experienced Zen meditation and mindfulness practice on three continents. In Europe and America I was largely surrounded by people with spiritual motivations. Although they'd rarely articulate it, they aspired to be like the great enlightened Zen masters of old.

In Japan it was a little different. Among the people I met, idealistic and spiritual motivations were not absent – my teacher, Shinzan Roshi himself, was a prime example of the quest for the ultimate, and often pointed out to me that the journey continued to deepen into his 60s and then into his 70s.

But as mentioned above, there were other intentions too. Probably the majority of people who came to join in Zen practice simply wanted to feel better, perhaps to be in a stronger position to navigate modern society. Some were looking for the grounded confidence and charisma that is a by-product of Zen meditation; others sought a quietening of their anxiety and fears. We occasionally welcomed people who had almost completely withdrawn from society (a type of person called *hikikomori* in Japanese), who were seeking to use Zen to create a bridge back to the everyday world. Zen master Shinzan welcomed them all, regardless of their aims, and worked tirelessly to help them achieve good health, happiness and a basis for success in their lives.

He often told me stories of how his own teacher, the great Zen master Itsugai, helped many people. A headline example was one of Japan's greatest ever baseball players who, having lost his mojo, regained championship form through Zen practice.

Zen master Shinzan is far from the only Japanese Zen teacher involved in the wellbeing aspects of mental cultivation. Rev. Takafumi Kawakami at Shunkō-in in Kyoto has had great success in teaching Zen meditation and mindfulness for a healthier and happier life, and even has a TedX talk on the subject.[7] He also has a book in Japanese entitled *Zen for Business Elites*.[8] Kenzo Maeda of Tokyo temple Kannon-ji runs Zen mindfulness experience programmes. Hironori Kawano is master of Rinko-ji temple in Yokohama, and also a practising

---

7   See www.youtube.com/watch?v=gDMOc_WCTWo

8   Kawakami, T. (2016) *Zen for Business Elites*. Tokyo: Kadokawa Shoten. Available at www.amazon.co.jp/dp/4041032768

psychiatrist trained in mindfulness modalities. These are just three examples.

There are so many books about Zen in English these days that I almost hesitate to attempt another one. While I've not read all of them, I haven't found a single book that brings this Zen tradition of meditative wellbeing to the Western world. However, I've seen for myself that there is considerable demand for its life-changing results.

I am aware that some might consider the profound spiritual insights of Zen to be more elevated and deserving of respect than these wellbeing-orientated processes. Shinzan Roshi never thought this way. As mentioned, in his temple, he always had meditators, whatever their motivation, practise side by side. He laid great stress on this togetherness and often mentioned its importance when explaining his view of life. He saw society as becoming increasingly atomised and fragmentary, and he passionately believed that every dimension of Zen meditation and mindfulness could be beneficial for the wellbeing and harmony of society. This is why he often said, 'Zen is not a religion.' In his view religions throughout history had caused division and conflict. Having experienced the devastation of a world war, he desperately wanted Zen to be a force for unity and peace.

After I was named Shinzan Roshi's successor I began to teach, primarily in the UK. Alongside the work with those seeking awakening, I, too, advocated the health and wellbeing modes of Zen practice. In fact, they came first.

I returned to England in June 2007. With no money or support or connections to speak of, I didn't really know where to start. So I decided to walk. The plan was simply to live on donations of food. At dawn on 21 June, midsummer morning, I set out northwards from St Catherine's Point on the

Isle of Wight, heading for Scotland. At about 9.30 a car pulled up beside me, the window came down and a voice asked, 'Are you Daizan?' I said I was. 'I heard about you on Isle of Wight Radio,' she continued. 'Will you teach me to meditate?' When I agreed she pulled the car into the side of the lane and I sat her down on the verge, using my rucksack as her meditation cushion. I taught her a breathing meditation for combating stress, the same as you have in this book.

After the walk ended on the north coast of Scotland, I created an eight-week programme for those wanting to explore Zen practice for health, wellbeing and optimal function, and a parallel programme for those interested in *satori*, or awakening Zen. Between then and now, together with the Zenways course leader team, I have trained over 50 Zen meditation and mindfulness teachers who have shared these programmes in the UK, US, Middle East, Japan and mainland Europe.

As mentioned before, Professor Maryanne Martin of the University of Oxford's Department of Experimental Psychology and Dr Barbara Jikai Gabrys have been studying the effects of the programme we're about to explore. They've found that students experience a significant decrease in perceived stress, together with a decrease in anxiety, plus increases in levels of awareness and satisfaction with life.[9]

This book gives you exactly the same techniques and insights you would learn on one of our live eight-week courses. It works as a self-study manual. If you can, however, I recommend using it in conjunction with a teacher so you get personal guidance and feedback. I know that this isn't always possible, so Sarah and I have tried to make the book the next best thing. In solitary practice, one of the key things you miss is a connection

---

9   See https://zenways.org/meditation-mindfulness-teacher-training

with fellow meditators, so we have included some case studies – people from various backgrounds who share their stories of the impact of Zen meditation and mindfulness practice on their lives.

So what are you actually going to gain from this book?

In answering that we need some definitions. First, let's look at the term 'meditation'. In certain quarters, meditation means to think on or around something, to chew it over. That's not how we're going to use the term here, though.

These days, meditation is typically thought of as mental cultivation. Meditation is fitness training for the mind, or more specifically, the attention. There are two broad types of meditation training, using a narrow or a broad focus.

Concentration means using a narrow focus point such as a mantra or an image. This type of practice is what people tend to think of when they view meditation as 'clearing the mind'. It progressively trains the mind to concentrate on the narrowed object of perception for a sustained period and exclude other experiences and perceptions. This is known in Sanskrit as *shamatha* (or *shi* in Japanese), which means 'calm abiding'.

We can contrast this with a wider inclusive focus leading to a clear seeing of how things are. This approach can be given the Sanskrit name *prajna* (Japanese, *hannya*), which means clear-seeing or wisdom.

The narrow-focus approach can lead to incredibly peaceful and restful states, but it's quite a training process to get to the higher levels. Also, while these states are generally beneficial, when you get off your meditation cushion and the afterglow has worn off, you're basically unchanged as a person.

The broad-focus way of meditation is different. You don't exclude any of the thoughts, emotions, memories and other processes of life. Quite the opposite – you develop an inclusive state of awareness. In practice this often means that the meditation is less immediately pleasurable than the narrow-focus way. However, when we allow life to flow through us without suppression or interference, we gain a whole new perspective, and a clarity and freedom that is highly transferable to everyday life. This is simply impossible to achieve when your practice involves excluding large areas of experience.

This broad/narrow focus model is slightly misleading in that we're dealing with a spectrum of breadth rather than two points. Nevertheless, I think it's useful to contrast the general approaches.

There is also a range of inner-cultivation approaches, ancient and modern, that apply the imagination. These practices can be most usefully called visualisation rather than meditation. Zen doesn't make a strong feature of this kind of work, and we won't be examining it in this book.

The practices we're going to be engaging in here will definitely enhance your powers of concentration. However, our main emphasis will be on the more practical broad-focus meditative approach.

Now let's look at the term 'mindfulness'. Printed here is my teacher's calligraphy of the Japanese character *nen*, which represents the ancient Buddhist term for mindfulness. It is made up of two other characters – the top half is the character for *ima*, 'now', and below is the character for *shin*, 'mind or heart'.[10]

---

10   Although pictorially representing mindfulness so well, the term *nen* has a wide range of meanings these days, including sense, wish, attention and idea. In discourse about mindfulness meditation, you're more likely to encounter *kokoro ga mitsareteiru joutai* (*mindfulness in a meditative cultivation sense*).

In Zen master Thich Nhat Hanh's writings, he uses the term mindfulness 'to refer to keeping one's consciousness alive to the present reality'.[11]

Here's a story about mindfulness or every-minute Zen.

At the end of the 19th century, Nanin was one of the most eminent Zen masters in Japan. A new Zen teacher, Tenno, came through the rain-swept streets of Kyoto to pay the master a courtesy call. Not sure on what element of the teachings he might be tested, the young teacher sat down with the grand old man. Without preamble Nanin asked him, 'Before you came in here, did you place your umbrella on the left or right side of your sandals?' Tenno was at a loss. Realising that his moment-by-moment mindfulness needed maturing, he put aside his teaching qualification and studied under Nanin for six further years.

Sometimes people get the idea that mindfulness is a quality of enhanced self-consciousness, as if you put a security camera on your shoulder and monitor your every move. Certainly things can feel this way at the beginning, but this is not the intention, nor the goal. I think a clue to what a developed mindfulness practice looks like lies in the Buddha's original instructions. He refers to 'mindfulness of the body *in the body*... Mindfulness of the breath *in the breath*', and so on. Rather than splitting the attention and its object, we bring them together.

We can divide mindfulness into two broad types. There can be an internal focus, such as in the practice of mindfulness of your thoughts, or an external one, such as Tenno's placement of his umbrella and sandals. Both orientations are of value.

---

11   Nhat Hanh, T. (1987) *The Miracle of Mindfulness: A Manual on Meditation.* Boston, MA: Beacon Press, p.11.

We're living in a time in the West when the non-spiritual use of meditation and mindfulness have become popular, even fashionable. Health practitioner Jon Kabat-Zinn (who studied with Zen master Thich Nhat Hanh) did great work in opening this door when he showed how beneficial these practices can be for hospital patients suffering chronic pain. An avalanche of health-related meditation and mindfulness research has followed. We'll look at some of the pivotal insights in this book.

Arising out of this medical-inspired mindfulness approach have come new practices blending elements of Western psychotherapy with meditative practices from various world spiritual traditions, primarily Buddhist. We're living in exciting times. However, what we have here in this book has the great advantage of being practically time-tested. In this sense you're joining a tradition. Your job is simply to put it into practice.

The surge of contemporary interest in non-spiritual or secular meditation and mindfulness has arisen largely due to the health benefits. But, as hinted above, this field is actually wider than that. It's good to see that scientific research is gradually expanding to reveal that these practices are not just for sick people. We'll see how they can also help the healthy to go beyond normal functioning in many dimensions of their lives.

To get these benefits there is no particular worldview or belief system that you need to adopt. The methods themselves are simple, although their application may not always be easy. Pretty much wherever you feel you are in life, there is value for you here.

However, there are two groups of people for whom these practices won't work optimally. The first are those who aren't yet ready to commit. You don't need to spend hours every day on your meditation cushion, but for best results, a regular and ongoing engagement is essential. We've found that it works best if you can dedicate 30 minutes a day, every day, over eight weeks to your practice. Why is this regularity so central?

I'd explain it like this. You can think of meditation practice as similar to music practice – a little every day is more valuable than a whole heap once in a blue moon. If you practise the piano for half an hour every day, in a year you'll be playing Beethoven. A parallel type of development is possible with daily meditation.

Or we can compare mental culture and physical culture. The UK Government now advises people to exercise five times a week. I believe the research is at a level to justify an identical recommendation for meditation.

So just reading the book or doing a little intermittent practice is frankly selling yourself short. The real benefits lie in action – 30 minutes a day for eight weeks.

Second, if you suffer from schizophrenia, paranoia or other problems of this kind, you need very particular help for this work to be useful to you. Don't try to learn it out of a book. I recommend the work of psychiatrist Dr Russell Razzaque.[12] Russell has extensive experience in sharing meditation and mindfulness practices with people suffering extreme psychological distress, and is presently spearheading a visionary NHS project called 'Open Dialogue', drug-free psychiatry based in non-judgemental presence and mindfulness.

Apart from the two situations above, your way ahead is clear. If you find you are willing to engage daily with the practice, it doesn't matter how distracted or chaotic your mind is right now. These simple methods will work for you – just put in the time.

Over the past decade or so, working with new meditators, I've found that, initially, 30 minutes a day is quite a challenge for them, but it is nevertheless achievable. Some people get up a bit earlier than usual or sit in the car at work during lunchtime;

---

12 See www.mindfulpsychiatry.org

some have a meditation break instead of a tea break. With a bit of creativity, there are all sorts of ways to fit it in. When you make the effort and fit in this amount of practice, I can guarantee you'll feel some very real changes and establish a solid platform for going forward.

So the question is, are you willing to make a commitment and shift your priorities so that you can build in this 30 minutes of practice time every single day over the next eight weeks? I really recommend thinking seriously about this. Not only are we going for a critical volume of practice here; another key element to your success is building a habit. Repetition is the only way to get the habit momentum working for you. Through the process you will have good days and bad days, guaranteed. But the more the practice becomes a habit – something you just do, regardless of how you're feeling – the more able you become to gracefully ride out the ups and downs, not only in your meditation, but more importantly, in your life generally.

So think, are you ready to try everything? The bits you like and the bits you don't? Are you willing to postpone the immediate gratification of slobbing out in front of the TV (or even doing important jobs) in order to gain the lifelong benefits that you'll reap from a meditation and mindfulness practice? Be real with yourself. You might want to take a little time to think this through. Put this book down until you're ready to commit and get started.

In the 30 minutes you set aside each day, you'll not only be meditating; I also recommend taking the last five minutes to write in a meditation diary. All you need is a simple notebook. I'm never far away from mine. The most important part is the beginning.

When you feel ready to embark on your Zen meditation and mindfulness journey, turn to the first page of your notebook. Write down your intention and commitment. Maybe something like this: 'I undertake for the duration of my meditation course to faithfully practise to the best of my ability for 30 minutes every day. I will do my best to practise all of the subsidiary exercises. I make this undertaking of my own free will.' Actually putting it in writing makes your engagement more solid and real. I've found time and time again in my own life that writing down my goals and intentions makes them far more likely to actually happen.

From now on, going forward, please take a few minutes at the end of each meditation period to write in your diary. I suggest treating it as a brain dump. Simply allow anything and everything on your mind to be transferred on to the paper. In the process you can digest it and let it go. If there's any thinking-through the material that arises in your meditation, let it happen with your pen in your hand. This really helps the meditation period to remain non-analytical. Later on, when we start to incorporate elements of the practices into your daily life, you can record them in your meditation diary. Tracking practice elements like this powerfully helps the formation of new habits. Gradually you get to take control of your life and steer it in beneficial directions.

So now let's begin to practise. After establishing the physical alignment, we're going to explore a practice called the 'bodyscan'. This practice finds many forms in the world's awareness traditions. It simply involves moving the non-judgemental, present-moment attention through the body in a sequential way. The version of the practice here is a simplified version of a practice called *nanso no ho* (healing ointment meditation) taught in the 17th century by Zen master Hakuin. You can explore the original version of the practice in my book *Practical Zen*.[13]

---

13   Skinner, J.D. (2017) *Practical Zen: Meditation and Beyond*. London: Singing Dragon.

Meditation postures

The Buddha frequently spoke of the four postures of meditation. These are walking, standing, sitting and lying down. We'll look at other postures later, but start with meditation while lying down. I've studied the two major traditions of Japanese Zen, each of which emphasises a different lying posture. Try both and choose the one that is more comfortable for you.

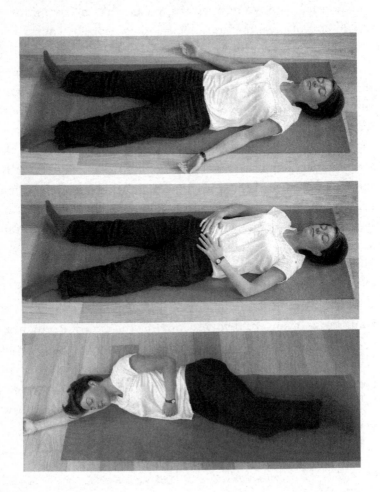

LYING ON YOUR BACK

We want your body aligned and yet relaxed. Many people find it beneficial to lie on a firm surface such as the floor rather than a soft bed. Experiment, and see what helps you. Extend your legs, allow your feet to fall out to the side, hands either folded on your belly or a little away from you but beside your body, with your palms facing up.

Lengthen your spine and neck. If it's more comfortable, you can have your feet planted on the floor with a support beneath your knees, which are pointed to the ceiling. You may find it more comfortable to have a small pillow for your head.

LYING ON YOUR SIDE

Traditionally we lie on the right side. Some people claim that this is because the heart is slightly to the left. Have your knees slightly bent and one leg on top of the other. Have your lower arm beneath you and supporting your head, your upper arm draped along the side of your body or, if you wish, resting on the floor in front of you. You may find it more comfortable to also have a cushion beneath your head and also possibly a rolled-up towel or a similar support beneath your waist. As in the lying on your back position, we want to create an extended and straight spine and neck, coupled with an overall quality of relaxation.

Once you've tried both of these positions and chosen one of them, we're ready to go. If it's not right for you to lie down just now, though, try the meditation practice sitting in a comfortable chair.

BODYSCAN MEDITATION

The bodyscan meditation practice has become widespread and popular for good reason. It powerfully aids you in developing an integration between body and mind. It keeps the mind moving, so for beginners, it's typically easier than single-focus point practice. There are many traditional sources for this type of practice. Our version comes from Japan and is distinctive in that the attention is always guided downwards through the body, encouraging grounding. You can start practising by reading through slowly from here as you move your attention through the body. Alternatively, you can follow along with the audio recording you'll find on the website associated with this book.[14] Once you're familiar with the practice, you'll find it's straightforward to do it without guidance. Take 25 minutes.

So, as we mentioned, you can practise this meditation (and all the others we'll be doing) standing, sitting, walking or lying down. There's a proverb in Japanese that says, 'The reclining person can't fall over.' We'll practise lying down, as this is usually easier than sitting positions.

Come into a comfortable position, lying on your back or on your side (see above). Make sure that your spine

---

14 Go to www.zenways.org/practical-zen-health.online and enter the password 'health'.

is long and straight, and also your neck. Adjust your position so that you can get as comfortable as possible. Allow your eyes to soften and rest downwards. You can close your eyes or keep them half-open, whichever is most comfortable for you. Have your mouth closed and your tongue resting against the roof of your mouth.

As much as you can, relax your body. Allow your breathing also to relax. When you relax like this, the breath tends to penetrate deeper into the body. Bring your attention to the lowest place in your body where you can feel this effortless breath. Perhaps right now you can feel the breath in your lower ribs, perhaps in your solar plexus, or maybe even down in your abdomen. Wherever for you is the lowest place reached by the breath without any strain or effort, that's where you rest your attention. Notice the sensations caused by the rising and sinking of the breath in this lowest place. What can you feel? Be aware and sensitive.

Now we're going to bring this mindfulness of sensations through the body.

First of all, bring the attention to the crown of your head, just becoming aware of what you can feel here, in the crown. Don't try to change anything, don't try to do anything; just be present with what you can feel here. It's normal to get distracted; just gently bring the mind back. You might feel a lot of sensations, or maybe not so much. If there's absolutely nothing at all, gently rest a hand here and notice the feeling of the contact.

And now bring your awareness to your forehead. Be simply present, aware. And now to the left side of your head, above your ear. The right side of your head, and the rear side of your head, behind your forehead.

Again, if you're not feeling any sensations, rest a hand in these places.

Bring your awareness now to your eyes, first your left eye, then your right eye; then your right ear, the back of your head in line with your ears, your left ear; bring your awareness to your nose, moving downwards through your body all the time; just be present, aware of how things are in your nose.

And now down again, be aware; around your mouth, your right jaw, the back of your head at the base of your skull, your left jaw. Move your awareness down again to your throat at the front, not doing anything, not changing anything, just aware. All the transformation you need comes simply from your awareness. Move your awareness to the right side of your neck, at the level of your throat, the back of your neck, the left side of your neck; move your awareness down again to the top of your chest at the front, to your right shoulder, the top of your back, your left shoulder; just be present, just simply aware.

Move your awareness down again, moving always downwards to the area of your chest at the level of your heart, slightly to your left, then the right side of your chest, under your right arm, your upper back on this level, under your left arm, becoming aware of your arms themselves, your right upper arm, your left upper arm, moving your awareness down into the lower part of your chest cavity, first on the left side, and now the right side, roughly at the level of your elbow, your back on this level, the left side of your body on the level of your elbow, your solar plexus, the right side of your abdomen, the right side of your body, the rear side of your body on this level, the left side of your body, your left abdomen.

Becoming aware of your elbow on your right side, on your left side, simply be present, simply be aware; move your awareness down again to the level of your navel, just being present, just being aware what's here at the front of your body, the right side of your body at the level of your navel, the rear side of your body, the left side of your body.

Move your awareness down again to the level of your pubic bone in your lower belly; just be present, be aware; now the right side of your body at this level, the rear of your body, your lower back, the left side of your body; move your awareness to your right lower arm, your left lower arm, move your awareness down again to the level of your pelvis at the front of your body, move your awareness to your right hip, the rear of your body at this level, your left hip. Distraction might happen now and again. Don't worry – just bring your mind back and continue.

Move your awareness down again to your right thigh, first the front, then the right side, the rear side of your right upper leg, the left side, moving your awareness to your left thigh, first the front of your upper leg, the right side, the rear side, the left side of your left upper leg; move your awareness, your presence, to your right wrist – what happens when an area comes into your awareness like this? Move your awareness to your right palm, the back of your hand, your right thumb, your index finger, middle finger, ring finger, little finger.

Move this attention to your left wrist, the palm of your hand, the back of your hand, your left thumb, your index finger, your middle finger, your ring finger, your little finger; move your presence, your awareness, down to your right knee, first the front of your knee, the right side of your knee, the back of your knee, then the left side of your knee; move your awareness to your left knee, the right side of your knee, the rear side of your knee, the left side of your knee; move your awareness down again, to your right lower leg, the front of your leg, the right side of your leg, the rear side of your leg, the left side of your leg; move your awareness to your left lower leg, the right side of your leg, the rear side, the left side and back to the front; move your awareness down again to your right ankle, first the front of your ankle, the right side, the rear of your ankle, the left side, back again to the front; move your awareness down to your left ankle, the front of your ankle, the right side, the rear of your ankle and the left side.

Move your awareness to your right foot, the topside of your foot, your right heel, the sole of your foot, your right big toe, your second toe, your third toe, your fourth toe, your fifth toe, moving this presence, this awareness, to your left foot, the topside of your foot, the left heel, the sole of your foot, your left big toe, your second toe, your third toe, your fourth toe, your fifth toe.

Now move your attention again up to the crown of your head, letting your awareness just sweep down through your body, perhaps a little faster now, a little more easily, through from the crown of your head all the way through and over your face, your head, your neck, over your shoulders, your chest, your upper back, down through your upper arms, down through your mid-back, your abdomen, your elbows, your lower arms, your hands, down through your pelvis, into your legs, down through your upper legs, your knees, your lower legs, your ankles, your feet, that's right.

As you become aware of all these areas you may find your awareness can slip down through the body even more readily, even more easily, just letting this happen very naturally, and now, allowing your awareness to be generalised through your whole body, particularly allowing yourself to be aware of any places of any kind of discomfort, tension, stress, anything that's not 100 per cent how it might be; allowing these areas to be held in this gentleness, in this curiosity, this presence. Don't try to change anything; just be aware, be present; the changes come when they're ready, and even if they don't come, that's fine too.

Now return your attention to the breath, to the lowest place in your body where you can feel sensations caused by the rising and sinking of your breath. Stay here for a few breaths and let things settle.

Now gently become aware of your fingers, your toes; gently start to move your fingers and your toes, and when you're ready, give the body a good stretch and come up to sitting.

Your meditation diary

Now open up your meditation diary. Pick up your pen and just write for five minutes. Splurge out whatever comes to mind. You don't need any censorship or editing, just write. Have the very soft intention to write about your practice, but if other things come up too, just get them down. Once you've done five minutes, put down your pen, close your diary and get on with your day.

Week One homework

For the first week, take 25 minutes each day to do your bodyscan meditation followed by five minutes writing in your meditation diary. If you want to use the audio recording, please go right ahead,[15] or you can practise unaccompanied. Don't worry too much about trying to evaluate how well you're doing. Just make sure you're practising every single day, and be assured that you're creating a better, healthier future for yourself.

Case study: Speech and language therapist
Name: Johanna Barclay
Lives: London

My first encounter with the body-scan meditation was a revelation.

Life before meditation was much more head-centred. I believed I knew my body and that I was feeling as much as there was to feel. But as soon as I did the bodyscan, what I realised was that there was so much more to experience and so much to be curious about.

What came out of that was the realisation that all these sensations are on the move, and one day to the next there's always something different to be interested in. There were parts of the body that didn't have much feeling to them at the beginning, but now the awareness

---

15 Go to www.zenways.org/practical-zen-health.online and enter the password 'health'.

seems to be penetrating to the depth of the bones. I'm finding I can feel into the bones and perhaps even the bone marrow.

This has brought me a much deeper sense of aliveness and also an appreciation of the fragility of life. I've found this sense of fragility has brought a greater kindness and compassion towards whatever arises, and for me this is what makes this practice special. It's not just an intellectual investigation; it's actually much more well rounded than that.

I think as I've become more aware of my own body, I tend to look more closely at other people too. More than that, it seems that the greater kindness you develop towards yourself spills out into your relationships too.

For me, there's still lots to explore. I think it's a practice you come back to and it keeps on giving. It's mostly a matter of remembering to do it. So, for example, at work, I changed my computer password to something that reminded me to do some practice. I'm also getting better at remembering when something happens and I feel a bit unsettled to do a short practice.

I've noticed how, in interactions, I sense how other people feel, using the body as a sort of antenna. I'm also increasingly noticing how I might absorb emotions and feelings from other people. The more I detect these things, the more I can live skilfully.

CHAPTER 2

Letting Go of Stress

'Seven times down; eight times up.'

– Japanese proverb, frequently quoted by Zen master Shinzan

We're going to look at stress, but before we do, just take a moment to settle more comfortably. Relax your body. Bring your attention to the crown of your head and then take ten seconds or so to send a wave of awareness down through the body, from your crown to your feet. Just check in; notice how you are right now. Do the same things two more times.

You've spent less than a minute doing this; notice the effects. We'll do more with this later. Now let's look at stress.

It's no secret that stress is the number one killer in our modern, fast-paced world. More than that, the American Medical Association notes that stress is implicated in 60–90 per cent of physician visits.[1]

When I was studying in a Zen temple in Japan we regularly used to have stressed-out salarymen or executives come to stay,

---

1   Avey, H., Matheny, K.B., Robbins, A. and Jacobson, T.A. (2003) 'Health care providers' training, perceptions, and practices regarding stress and health outcomes.' *Journal of the National Medical Association 95*, 9, 833, 836–845.

hoping to prevent their health breaking down. There was dark talk of *karōshi*, where employees literally work themselves to death. We also had visits from *freeters*, people who opt for part-time work to avoid the ruthless rat race, but then end up locked into stressful, insecure and unfulfilling positions. Zen master Shinzan used to say, 'We have to show them, *nana korobi, ya oki*,' meaning, 'Seven times down; eight times up.' He was referring to a Daruma, a type of Japanese doll with a weighted base that regardless how it is rocked always comes to rest upright. Before we explore how to develop this kind of resilience, let's look a little more at how stress affects us on emotional, physical and mental levels.

Stress can be caused by both external and internal factors. External causes can range from an overwhelming workload to a challenging romantic relationship. Internally, stress can be caused by factors like cycles of rumination and negative thoughts. A certain amount of stress keeps us alert and motivated. Too much stress, however, leads to a miserable existence.

Worryingly, many of us have come to believe that it's normal to live with excessive stress. We can become numb to what we're doing to ourselves. Or we react to stress in a knee-jerk fashion by resorting to quick fixes. Doctors continue to prescribe more and more pills for anxiety and depression – both stress-related conditions. Health analysts Medco found that, over the 2000s, the proportion of US citizens on anxiety and behavioural medical prescriptions went up 22 per cent (with the number of young men taking prescriptions increasing by 43 per cent). While this avalanche of pill popping might alleviate symptoms in the short term, it's clearly not going to resolve the root causes of stress. Plus there's the problem of a range of unwanted side effects.

Let's dig into what stress actually is. The word 'stress' was popularised in the 1950s by Dr Hans Selye. He was studying animal behaviour and defined it as 'the nonspecific response of the organism to any pressure or demand'.[2] So *stress* is how your body and mind react to these demands, also called *stressors*. Selye and other leading researchers established that stress has a direct impact on the immune system. This, in turn, makes us more vulnerable to disease. The origins of the word 'disease' come from the old French word *desaise*, meaning 'lack of ease'. A wide range of illnesses result from failed attempts to adapt to stressful conditions.

So how exactly does this stress reaction manifest?

Stress makes most sense when we go back into our past. As a species, we've spent most of our time on this planet wandering in small groups on the great plains of Africa. In this setting, the stress reaction helped in survival.

Essentially, a stress reaction occurs in three stages:

1. The initial *fight, flight or freeze* reaction that mobilises the body for immediate action. For example, on encountering a predator we might fight it off, we might run away, or we might remain utterly still and try not to be noticed. Each of these reactions could give us a survival edge.
2. A *slower resistance* reaction. In this longer follow-up phase, the body is mobilising all its forces to enable us to get to safety and begin recovery.
3. *Exhaustion.* This sets in eventually if the body doesn't get to a place where rest and recovery can happen.

In the first stage the nervous system diverts energy to the muscles and organs needed for immediate survival. During this initial reaction, the body releases stress hormones, particularly adrenaline, heightening sense perceptions and

2   Selye, H. (1974) *Stress without Distress*. Philadelphia, PA: J.B. Lippincott Co, p.14.

creating hyperarousal so we can absorb as much information as possible. The heart output jumps and more blood is directed to the arms and legs. At the same time, blood flow to non-essential areas like the digestive and reproductive systems shuts down.

During the second, resistance, stage, the body releases cortisol and human growth hormone. Over a short period these hormones produce increased energy, help the body repair damaged cells and reduce inflammation.

In the third stage, if rest and recovery have not been possible, the body continues to produce large amounts of stress hormones. Prolonged exposure to these (especially cortisol) destroys healthy muscles, bones and cells and weakens the immune system.

So, if our stone-age ancestor is going about his daily business and suddenly a lion leaps out from behind a rock, his survival chances are enhanced if he stands and fights or runs away at maximum speed or freezes to stillness. The stress reaction is perfectly suited to his situation.

We also have access to a further response, often called the 'flop' response. When our system perceives the threat to be totally overwhelming (with no way of fighting or fleeing), we literally play dead. The system goes into shutdown and collapse. Many predators don't eat carrion, so playing dead would have given us a survival edge too.

Nowadays, however, things are different. We don't encounter hungry lions that often. And if we are in the middle of a stressful dressing-down from the boss, very likely the three worst responses would be to kill him, to run out screaming, or to play dead! So we have to learn how to manage these archaic stress responses.

As we all know, in day-to-day modern life we're rarely dealing with life or death situations. Rather, we typically experience an accumulation of minor stress reactions. We may well be dealing almost constantly with mild states of hyperarousal without many avenues to discharge the stress hormones. Then, as each small, irksome incident increases our stress load, our system is gradually undermined. Eventually our health starts to break down.

So what can we do to alleviate this? The good news is that we can change how we respond to stress. While we may or may not be able to change the stressor, we can learn to shift how we perceive and handle situations. Doing this will change what happens internally. With practice we can change our world.

We need to be realistic here. Stressors exist in a spectrum. On the upper end, strong enough stressors will kill us regardless of how mindful we are. Take the absence of oxygen as an example. On the other hand, some stressors are so mild they aren't really registered by the conscious mind. It's the huge mid-range of stressors where this work is most effective, but in what way?

According to Dr Jon Kabat-Zinn, in his book *Full Catastrophe Living*, 'You have the power to affect the balance point between your internal resources for coping with stress and the stressors that are an unavoidable part of modern living.'[3]

So, the same event is more stressful for someone who has fewer resources. Building up our inner and outer sources of resilience is an effective way of combating stress. Friends, family, teachers and our environment can provide vital external resources. Meanwhile, our beliefs, our mental skills and our view of ourself are all valuable inner resources. These are important for happiness and wellbeing.

---

3   Kabat-Zinn, J. (2013) *Full Catastrophe Living* (revised edn). London: Piatkus, p.293.

Right back to the time of the Buddha, we find claims that these practices can develop warrior-like inner resources for dealing with the struggles of life (and, in fact, they were used that way by samurai back in pre-modern Japan). How would this work? Well, first, our practice can provide an oasis of calm and relaxation in which we can recuperate and recharge. And second, it develops awareness so we can perceive clearly what we are going through. This is critical because there is a huge difference between conscious and unconscious stress.

Hakuin, the great Japanese Zen master, wrote, 'Buddhas are like water and ordinary people are like ice.' Our mindfulness, our awareness, is like the warm sunlight, which begins the process of melting away the stress.

At the heart of East Asian philosophies like Buddhism and Taoism is the conviction that change is universal. We have some of this stance in Western culture too. The Greek philosopher Heraclitus taught that 'you never step into the same river twice'. There is nothing in life that doesn't slowly or quickly go through a process of change. In fact, if we investigate this concept on a deeper level, we can experience a perspective where we see that there are no fixed things, just processes in motion, and that includes us.

Quantum physics also opens a window into this kind of viewpoint. Even the most solid-appearing objects and substances are found, on a microscopic scale, to be intensely dynamic. In the modern world, this ungraspable dynamism is very relevant to day-to-day experience. Experts talk about the 'RoCoRoC principle', the rate of change of the rate of change, which is apparently doubling every ten years. If you reflect, it's clear that our own bodies, relationships and roles are constantly changing.

Learning how to surf the ocean of change rather than fight it is critical to our wellbeing. In *Full Catastrophe Living*,

Jon Kabat-Zinn states, 'The ultimate effect on our health of the total psychological stress we experience depends in large measure on how we come to perceive change itself in all its various forms, and how skilful we are in adapting to continual change while maintaining our own inner balance and sense of coherence.'[4]

When we start living mindfully, we improve our relationship with change. Rather than change being the enemy, we become able to relax and enjoy the ever-changing quality of experience. Over time, and with practice, our realisation of change in every dimension makes the universe seem like a vast symphony, and moment by moment, we arise as a newborn being in a newborn world.

Making friends with change is a great medium-term goal. We get there by focusing on experience now. And it's in the present moment that we can deal with stress. We all have a range of stressors – some very transitory, like worrying about whether that child on the street might step in front of your car; others are more long term (and ongoing), such as paying our yearly tax bill. Some stressors are external – the freezing cold rainstorm that suddenly lands on you. Some are internal, such as the strange lingering headache that has you looking up symptoms on the internet. When we experience a stressor, internal or external, the body and mind will react to it as if it's a threat.

As mentioned, in beginning our journey to stress relief the critical element is awareness. There's a natural tendency to want to avoid unpleasantness, but suppressing feelings doesn't stop their effects. Unconscious stress can lead to poor sleep, indigestion, chronic head and backaches, heart attacks, and

---

4   Kabat-Zinn, J. (2013) *Full Catastrophe Living* (revised edn). London: Piatkus.

so on. When our health starts to deteriorate, we become more fearful, and the whole situation becomes a vicious circle.

The avoidant person's coping mechanisms might include denial, distractions (including 'busyness and workaholism'), shopping, alcohol, drugs, gambling, exercise (both beneficial and excessive amounts) and food (overeating or undereating). Even meditation itself could be an avoidance mechanism.

In my teens, as I mentioned previously, Father Jack Madden taught me a meditation practice involving concentration on a syllable (an Indian sacred word). After some time I found myself more and more able to rest my attention on the concentration point. I began to feel great – deeply relaxed; peaceful like I'd never known peaceful. It was wonderful. But then, over time, I found myself spacing out, simply not dealing with things. I felt like I was floating in a cloud above it all. The technical term for this sort of experience is 'dissociation'. In a sense nothing was going wrong – the meditation was designed to induce this sort of thing. But I found myself uncomfortable with the results. I ended up quitting my practice, feeling that what I was achieving was just another form of avoidance.

None of the above solves the root cause of stress, and almost always the negative effects simply continue, masked by the distraction. And as we saw above, if left unresolved for long enough, stress leads to burnout, breakdown and long-term sickness.

So avoidance doesn't serve us. But what actually works? Jon Kabat-Zinn writes, 'The healthy alternative to being caught in this self-destructive pattern is to stop reacting to stress and to start responding to it.'[5] Reaction is largely unconscious; response is the path of awareness.

---

5   Kabat-Zinn, J. (2013) *Full Catastrophe Living* (revised edn). London: Piatkus.

How do we work with this greater awareness that Zen meditation and mindfulness practice make available?

First, apply your awareness within the physical stillness of your practice time. Simply be present with the tension or butterflies in your stomach or whatever stress-related sensation arises. Just be with it. You're lying on the floor and moving your attention through the body and you land on it. Good. Now all you need to do is simply be here. Don't try to change it or make it go away or suppress it. Simply be with what's here. Shinzan Roshi, my Zen teacher, constantly uses the Japanese term *nari kiru* to express what we do here. *Nari* means literally 'become' and *kiru* means 'totally' or 'completely'. So once you find the tension or stress, don't separate yourself from it; quite the opposite, be *with* it, *become* it. In that moment there is no gap between you and the sensation.

Perhaps we can explore this right now. Is there somewhere in your body right now that might be exhibiting a stress reaction? You might find tension or discomfort of some kind. If there is, turn your attention towards the feeling and just be here with it. If you can, sit right in the middle of the physical stress effect rather than being on the outside looking at it. Notice what happens. We mentioned previously that change is universal. This physical symptom, too, slowly or quickly, will change. It might dissolve or move somewhere else; it might turn to heat. Trains of memory or emotion might start to come. It might even seem that it intensifies. Whatever's going on, just stay with it. Awareness is a great accelerator of the change process. Don't worry if the stress effect doesn't seem to be changing immediately; the most important thing, the revolutionary step, is that you're here, you're aware, you're allowing. Don't try to impose your own timescale. You can come back tomorrow if necessary. You can come back the day after. From now on, every time you encounter the symptoms of stress in your body in your meditation, you can do this, you can just be with them and notice what happens.

Through developing this attitude in the stillness of your meditation you'll become dramatically more able to deal with stress in the midst of activity. How do we do this? It's basically the same process. In a time of stress, try to remain centred and aware. The more aware you are, the more you will be able to distinguish between the stressor and your response. The stressor has reality and there may be some way of changing that reality – moving away from it or attenuating it in some way.

The stress you experience also has its reality. Be aware of your thoughts, feelings and sensations. Simply and unreservedly be with them. This awareness provides a freedom. As we know, you don't have to run away from these thoughts, feelings and sensations, and nor do you have to react to them in any particular way. This presence reduces the strength of your reaction, reduces your stress, even to the point where you start to find that many things no longer push your buttons.

Establishing this non-reactive space will also reduce the time you need to recover from stressful situations. Things will release so much more easily.

Naturally, it takes time to develop this stability and awareness. That's why we practise meditation every day. Your practice in stillness will inform your practice in life. Over time your awareness strengthens, making it much easier to shift from a stress reaction to a stress response in the heat of the moment.

As mentioned, stress-related illnesses are the number one killer, so we can truthfully say that this Zen approach can literally save your life. It will also provide you with a huge sense of liberation.

So when you next encounter a stressful situation, don't act out and don't suppress your feelings. Instead, remain aware. Allow thoughts, feelings and sensations to arise and to pass, and act as appropriately as you can. This is the path from stress to freedom.

BODYSCAN MEDITATION

You've already done a week of practice with the bodyscan meditation. In developing this eight-week course we've found that most people do best with two full weeks of this method. This week we're going to develop last week's practice a little further.

The Buddha said that 'mindfulness centred on the body leads to a happy life here and now and to the culmination of wisdom and end of suffering'. The bodyscan meditation practice works on many deep levels. Although you can practise this meditation standing, sitting, walking or lying down, we're going to continue working with the lying positions. Like last week, we take 25 minutes.

By now you'll be very familiar with the practice. In continuing I recommend you choose one of four options:

- Read through the text to remind you, put the book down, set your timer, and practise the bodyscan meditation based on your memory.
- Listen to the guided meditation soundtrack as you practise.[6]

---

6   Go to www.zenways.org/practical-zen-health.online and enter the password 'health'.

- Set your timer and actually practise along with reading the text.
- If you feel familiar enough with the process, based on what you've done up to now, simply put the book down, set your timer and jump straight into bodyscan practice.

Once you've decided which of the four options you're going to choose, come into a lying position, on your back or on your side, whichever is more comfortable for you. As much as is possible, make sure your spine is long and straight, your neck as well. Adjust your position so that you can become as relaxed as possible, but don't try to force anything. Allow your eyes to rest downwards; you can then close them fully or rest them half open along the line of your nose, whichever is most comfortable for you. Have your mouth closed and your tongue resting against the roof of your mouth.

Bring your attention to your breath. Notice the deepest place in your body where you feel the natural, effortless rising and sinking. You may find you can feel it in your lower ribs, or perhaps in your solar plexus, or even maybe in your belly. Simply rest your attention on what you can feel – the sensations generated by this rising and sinking. You're not trying to change anything or control anything. Simply be present with what is.

Now, we're going to move this presence or awareness through the body.

First, bring the attention to the crown of your head in the way you've become familiar. Just become aware of the crown of your head. Again, don't try to change anything, don't try to do anything; simply be present with what you can sense in the crown of your head.

And now bring your awareness to your forehead. Just be present and aware. And now to the left side of your head, above your ear; the right side of your head, and the rear side of your head, behind your forehead. And bring your awareness now to your eyes, first your left eye, your right eye, then your right ear, the back of your head in line with your ears, your left ear; bring your awareness to your nose, moving downwards through your body all the time; just be present, aware of how things are in your nose.

And now down again, aware; around your mouth, your right jaw, the back of your head at the base of your skull, your left jaw. Move your awareness down again to your throat at the front. Not doing anything, not changing anything, just aware. All the transformation you need comes simply from your awareness. Move your awareness to the right side of your neck at the level of your throat, the back of your neck, the left side of your neck; move your awareness down again to the top of your chest at the front, to your right shoulder, to the top of your back, your left shoulder, just be present, simply aware.

Move your awareness down again, moving always downwards to the area of your chest at the level of your heart, slightly to your left, the right side of your chest, under your right arm, your upper back on this level, under your left arm, becoming aware of your arms themselves, your right upper arm, your left upper arm, moving your awareness down to the lower part of your chest cavity, first on the left side, then on the right side, and now the right side of your body, roughly at the level of your elbow, your back on this level, the left side of your body at the level of your elbow, your solar plexus, the right side of your abdomen, the right side of your body, the rear side of your body on this level, the left side of your body, your left abdomen. Becoming aware of your elbow on your right side, on your left side, simply be present, simply aware; move your awareness down again to the level of your navel, just being present, just being aware what's here at the front of your body, the right side of your body on the level of your navel, the rear side of your body, the left side of your body.

Move your awareness down again to the level of your pubic bone in your lower belly, just be present, aware; now the right side of your body at this level, the rear of your body, your lower back, the left side of your body; move your awareness to your right lower arm, your left lower arm; move your awareness down again to the level of your pelvis at the front of your body; move your awareness to your right hip, the rear of your body at this level, your left hip.

Move your awareness down again to your right upper leg, first the front, the right side, the rear side of your right upper leg, the left side; move your awareness to your left upper leg, first the front, the right side, the rear side, the left side of your left upper leg; move your awareness, your presence, to your right wrist – what happens when an area comes into your awareness like this? Move your awareness to your right palm, the back of your hand, your right thumb, your index finger, middle finger, ring finger, little finger.

Move your awareness to your left wrist, the palm of your hand, the back of your hand, your left thumb, your index finger, your middle finger, your ring finger, your little finger; move your presence, your awareness, down to your right knee, first the front of your knee, the right side of your knee, the back of your knee, the left side of your knee; move your awareness to your left knee, the right side of your knee, the rear side of your knee, the left side of your knee; move your awareness down again, to your right lower leg, the front of your leg, the right side of your leg, the rear side, the left side of your leg; move your awareness to your left lower leg, the right side of your leg, the rear side, the left side and back to the front; move your awareness down again to your right ankle, first the front of your ankle, the right side, the rear of your ankle, the left side, back again to the front; move your awareness down to your left ankle, the front of your ankle, the right side of your ankle, the rear side and the left side.

Move your awareness to your right foot, the topside of your foot, your right heel, the sole of your foot, your right big toe, your second toe, your third toe, your fourth toe, your fifth toe; move this presence, this awareness, to your left foot, the topside of your foot, the left heel, the sole of your foot, your left big toe, your second toe, your third toe, your fourth toe, your fifth toe.

Now move your awareness again up to the crown of your head, letting your awareness just sweep down through your body, perhaps a little faster now, a little more easily, through from the crown of your head, all the way through and over your face, your head, your neck, over your shoulders, your chest, your upper back, down through your upper arms, down through your mid-back, your abdomen, your elbows, your lower arms, your hands, down through your pelvis, to your legs, down through your upper legs, your knees, your lower legs, your ankles, your feet, that's right.

Now accelerate this process a little bit. We're going to practise what we call the one-breath bodyscan. On your inhale, return your focus to the crown of your head. As you breathe out, move this attention downwards through the body to the toes in a smooth flow of awareness. Inhale, return to the crown, exhale, moving the awareness downwards. Repeat this process several times.

Now allow your awareness to generalise through your whole body, particularly allowing yourself to be aware of any places of any kind of discomfort, tension, stress, anything that's not 100 per cent how it might be, allowing these areas to be held in this gentleness, in this curiosity, this presence of your awareness.

Don't try to change anything; just be aware, be present; the changes come when they're ready, and even if they don't come, that's fine too. When you're in this quality of awareness, your relationship to all these things changes in a very beneficial way.

Now return your attention to the breath, to the lowest place in the body you can detect the sensations generated by the effortless rising and sinking of your spontaneous breath. Rest your mindfulness here for a few breaths.

And now move your awareness to the edges of your body; become aware of your fingers, your toes, gently starting to move into your fingers, your toes, gently, gently, allow yourself a really good, deep stretch, a really good stretch, allowing your body to get ready to carry on with the next thing.

Week Two homework

Practise the bodyscan meditation for 25 minutes every day and take five minutes to write in your meditation diary immediately afterward. Don't try to edit or censor – just write out whatever's coming. Also take a few moments to note down any particular stressors that you recently encountered. Just by bringing them to your awareness you'll start to get a clearer perspective on your responses.

Case study: Investment banker

Name: Curtis Perkins
Lives: New Jersey, USA

I became interested in meditation at a time when my life was spiralling out of control. I worked as an investment banker in a highly pressurised environment brimming with office politics – backstabbing and mind games occurred almost every day. Then, out of the blue, I was made redundant. Even though I was able to escape a toxic workplace, my stress levels shot up even further.

And all my worst fears surfaced. Having 'unemployed' as a job title reduced my sense of identity and self-esteem. As a man, I felt inadequate. Initially, I remained in a state of denial. Then I retreated too far into myself – internalising my feelings of shame and guilt – and this became a vicious circle.

As a father to three children, I wanted to provide them with the best possible college education and I didn't want to let them down. Also, my mother's health was seriously declining and I was worried that she wouldn't be able to receive adequate care. I also put my wife under pressure too – while she runs a small business, her income alone wasn't sufficient to cover our mortgage, tax bills and the educational fees.

That's when I realised I desperately needed an outlet and so started learning Zen meditation. My teacher gave me practical tips that immediately reduced my anxiety levels. The bodyscan meditation helps me to be aware of my state of being and to begin living in the present moment. When I am fully present, I no longer fret about the future. I'm still learning to master this, but every time I move my attention to the here and now, I feel much happier. Meditation has also taught me that I'm not always in control of everything and that's fine. Perhaps most importantly I've realised that my self-worth is not dependent on my earning power.

I've been practising meditation now for almost a year and my thought process is far more positive. Besides securing a well-paid part-time job, I now have time to pursue my passions in life – I'm in a recreational basketball team and do regular circuit training, plus I enjoy sketching and painting. For me, having an ongoing Zen practice has been a real lifesaver.

CHAPTER 3

Overcoming Physical Pain

'Pain is inevitable, suffering is optional.'

– Alcoholics Anonymous slogan

As you read this, settle your body comfortably. As much as you can, allow your trunk to take on its natural uprightness. Relax the body and notice how the breath naturally relaxes too. Lower your eyes and either keep the eyelids a little lifted, or close the eyes fully. Rest your attention on your natural, relaxed breath at the lowest place you can feel it, perhaps your lower chest or even down into your belly. Begin to mentally count the breath – in-breath, mentally count one, out-breath, two and so on, up to ten. Don't try to block or reduce any thoughts or other processes of life, just allow them to be as they are. Simply centre your attention on the sensation of the rising and sinking of your breath at the lowest place you can sense it. After you've counted to ten, allow your eyes to lift. Notice how you feel. Now continue reading.

There's a little incident that throws light on the issue of pain. After the Buddha realised enlightenment through his meditation practice, he spent over 30 years teaching and travelling in northern India, living very simply and sometimes sleeping in rough conditions. Late on in his life he suffered back pain. Once, his assistant, Ānanda, was giving the Buddha a massage, and commented on how age was wrinkling and bending his body. The Buddha agreed and said, 'I spit on you, old age.'[1] Some time later he continued the theme:

> Ānanda, I am old now, worn out, great in years, having gone the pathway of life well past its prime, I have reached the point of life which is now eighty years of age... Ānanda, whenever the Tathāgata [the Buddha] is not attending to any outward forms – feelings cease, and he enters into and abides in a collected repose of the mind; thus at that time, Ānanda, the body of the Tathāgata is comfortable.[2]

These exchanges highlight some key points about physical pain. First, it doesn't matter how enlightened you get, you are going to experience pain in your life, at least at some point, that much is guaranteed!

But there's something else in this little anecdote. Meditation can greatly reduce pain levels. This insight has come into sharp focus in recent years, and we'll discuss why shortly.

But before we do, let's take another perspective. When you are in the early stages of establishing your practice, it may feel like meditation increases physical discomfort. If you are tight in your body or have been sitting for some time, it's common to

---

1   Jara Sutta: Old Age, SN 48.41, PTS: S v 216. Translated from the Pali by Thanissaro Bhikku. See www.accesstoinsight.org/tipitaka/sn/sn48/sn48.041.than.html

2   Mahaparinibbana Sutta, Digha Nikaya 16.13. See https://dhammawheel.com/viewtopic.php?t=13429

feel pain in your hips and sometimes in your back and shoulders. When anyone sits still for long enough, the body starts to hurt.

Almost always, the pain you experience in meditation is temporary and leads to no harm. Naturally it's vital to be sensible with this and listen to your body. If in doubt about whether any damage is occurring, adjust your position to be more comfortable. But if you're dealing with passing aches and pains, you can treat them as a great learning opportunity.

So how do we deal with pain? Remember that we mentioned the two types of meditation:

- Narrow focus. In this type of practice we avoid pain by tuning out the unpleasantness. We simply put the mind somewhere else. Strong concentration practice refines and narrows consciousness. We simply put our focus exclusively on our object of meditation. A parallel situation might be when you're watching a good film and naturally you tend not to dwell on pain or discomfort in your body. You're involved in the storyline and simply don't notice the pain so much. I mentioned in the previous chapter how my initial efforts at meditation, focusing on a sacred syllable, created this tuning-out effect.

- Broad focus. Here you tune in. In this opposite approach you allow all the experiences of life to arise and pass within the space of your awareness. When pain arises, you can even make it your object of mindfulness. You just pay attention without excluding anything, however unpleasant it might be. You can even develop a welcoming, friendly attitude to the discomfort. Just allow it to be present and be with it. Don't try to change it or push it away; simply allow. This was what I was taught by my Zen teachers when I came back to meditation practice in my early 20s. Nothing was to be avoided. It was a matter of facing reality directly.

We've spent the last two weeks developing a greater level of awareness of bodily sensations. You may already be sensing how this mindfulness of sensations can shift your perspective. We mentioned previously the universal nature of change. When you become present with physical pain, you will experience this directly. Either immediately, or after some time, the discomfort will begin to change. It may dissolve or soften; it may intensify for a time; it may move to another place; it may become heat. All kinds of things can happen. What is guaranteed is that as you pay attention to pain, it transforms. You'll also discover that as your experience of the changeable nature of physical pain develops, your relationship to pain also shifts. No longer are you simply a passive victim; you have some power in the situation.

When pain arises, together with the direct experience of the pain itself, there is frequently a mental commentary. This mental aspect of pain is almost never helpful. When you centre your attention on the direct physical sensation of pain, you're far less likely to get pulled into emotional anguish, rumination, catastrophising and other mental baggage. The whole experience becomes much easier to handle.

So how specifically do we work with pain in our meditation? Of the two options outlined above, by far the most practical in my opinion is the second, the inclusive attitude. When you're practising, all kinds of feelings and sensations naturally arise and pass. Suppose there's a sense of pain that seems to persist. Treat this persistence as a call for help. If there's any possibility that damage is happening (particularly in your knees if you're on the floor), please move. Otherwise simply move your attention to the physical location of the pain. Approach it gently and respectfully. If you feel able, simply be with the pain. Your awareness is open, nothing is excluded, but as much as you are able, maintain the centre of your attention on the centre of the pain. You're not trying to change anything here, you're not trying to make anything happen; you're simply here with the pain as fully as you can be. Now your job is simply to stay here. If you do, the pain will change. The change may be immediate, it may take some time, even multiple meditation periods, but the pain will shift and the call on your attention will eventually not be there any more. Then you simply return your awareness to your regular object of meditation.

Occasionally, when you rest your attention in the pain like this, the discomfort increases. It may even seem to expand and engulf more of your body. If this happens to you, don't worry, nothing's going wrong. This is just a stage. If the pain gets too much, have a little break. You can approach this work at your own pace. If you are able to stay with the increasing pain, it will almost certainly release and dissipate. Again, it may take a little time before this happens.

While your Zen meditation and mindfulness practice will give you valuable practical experience of how to handle pain, the practice isn't a magical cure. As we noted, even the Buddha experienced pain. All human life contains some pain. What you gain from facing pain rather than avoiding it is a new confidence. Pain doesn't have to be something to fear.

How meditation changes pain experience is still something of a mystery. Indeed, pain itself and how we experience it is still not very well understood. Experimenters have found that processes like hypnosis and acupuncture reduce pain through activating the internal opioids, the body's natural painkiller hormones. Meditation seems to be different. Recent research has found that even when the internal painkiller system is shut down, a short course in meditation can reduce pain experience by up to 24 per cent.[3]

Brain imaging with meditators exposed to pain reveals that multiple brain mechanisms are activated. Which of these mechanisms are critical to meditation's unique effects has yet to be clarified. Dr Christopher Brown at the University of Manchester is currently investigating exactly this subject. At this early stage of the investigation, a certain perspective is gaining currency. Meditation helps your body and mind to deeply relax. The instinctive reaction to pain is to resist it. For example, when you have a back injury, the muscles around the injured area tend to tense up, forming a kind of splint preventing further damage. However, excessive muscle tension reduces blood flow to the affected area, slowing down the healing process. For both pain control and healing, managed relaxation of the sort that meditation produces seems to work better than tension.

It's worth remembering that when you meditate with pain, you don't need to stop any medical treatment you're receiving. There's no need to be a purist about the situation. Meditation and mindfulness practice combines well with almost any treatment therapy.

So rather than fighting or avoiding the pain, as much as possible, we relax with it. As we've seen, paradoxically, the attitude that is most transformative is one of acceptance. Simply be present with the reality of the situation. Thich Nhat Hanh, the Vietnamese Zen master, wrote a book I'd recommend called *The Miracle of Mindfulness*. It's in this accepting awareness that the miracles happen.

---

3   Zeidan, F., Adler-Neal, A.L., Wells, R.E., Stagnaro, E. *et al.* (2016) 'Mindfulness-meditation-based pain relief is not mediated by endogenous opioids.' *Journal of Neuroscience 36*, 11, 16 March, 3391–3397.

The first ground-breaking evidence for meditation being a therapeutically credible way of dealing with pain appeared in 1985 in the *Journal of Behavioral Medicine*.[4] Behind this work was American molecular biologist and Zen meditation practitioner Jon Kabat-Zinn and his team. Describing the origin of his work, Kabat-Zinn stated:

> What I wanted to do was bring together my work as a scientist and a Dharma practitioner in such a way that it would be really meaningful. Just doing molecular biology wasn't cutting the mustard for me. There was a long time when I didn't know what I wanted to do, but I did know what I didn't want to do. Then at a certain moment on a retreat, it came to me – literally, in like ten seconds. It was the whole thing. I saw that if this were successful, it would have influence and spread out to hospitals around the country and around the world. It would have lots of different potentialities way beyond medicine or psychology.[5]

Kabat-Zinn and his team established that chronic pain patients benefited from a ten-week course in Zen-influenced mindfulness meditation. Significant findings included reduced present-moment pain, negative body image, mood disturbance and psychological symptoms, like anxiety and depression.

---

4   Kabat-Zinn, J., Lipworth, L. and Burney, R.J. (1985) 'The clinical use of mindfulness meditation for the self-regulation of chronic pain.' *Journal of Behavioral Medicine 8*, 163.

5   Quoted in Fisher, D. (2010) 'Mindfulness and the cessation of suffering: An exclusive new interview with mindfulness pioneer Jon Kabat-Zinn.' *Lion's Roar*, 7 October. Available at www.lionsroar.com/mindfulness-and-the-cessation-of-suffering-an-exclusive-new-interview-with-mindfulness-pioneer-jon-kabat-zinn

Pain-related drug utilisation decreased and feelings of self-esteem increased. Men and women saw similar improvements, and the effects were not limited to any particular type of physical pain. A comparison group of pain patients did not show parallel improvements after receiving traditional treatment. Even more compelling was the discovery that improvements observed during this research were maintained up to 15 months post-course.[6] This research was significant. It introduced a new and proven means of pain control. But Kabat-Zinn himself sees a more profound significance. He believes that his work 'is the movement of the Dharma [the Buddhist teachings] into the mainstream of society'.[7]

Further pain-related research followed. Researchers from the Université de Montréal compared the experience of pain among experienced Zen practitioners with the experience of non-meditators. They found that the meditators had a considerably higher pain threshold. This was thought to be possibly due to slower breathing – meditators breathe about 12 breaths per minute versus an average of 15 breaths for non-meditators. Slower breathing has a number of effects including lowering the heart rate and blood pressure.[8]

A study on pain experience conducted at the University of Manchester[9] went inside the brain. The prefrontal cortex is

6   Kabat-Zinn, J., Lipworth, L. and Burney, R.J. (1985) 'The clinical use of mindfulness meditation for the self-regulation of chronic pain.' *Journal of Behavioral Medicine 8*, 163.

7   Shonin, E. (2015) 'This is not McMindfulness by any stretch of the imagination.' *The Psychologist*, 18 May. Available at http://thepsychologist.bps.org.uk/not-mcmindfulness-any-stretch-imagination

8   Grant, J.A. and Rainville, P. (2009) 'Pain sensitivity and analgesic effects of mindful states in Zen meditators: A cross-sectional study.' *Psychosomatic Medicine 71*, 106–114.

9   Brown, C.A. and Jones, A.K. (2010) 'Meditation experience predicts less negative appraisal of pain: Electrophysiological evidence for the involvement of anticipatory neural responses.' *The Journal of Pain 150*, 3, 428–438.

known to control thought processes when potential threats are perceived. The researchers found that, during anticipation of pain, advanced meditators showed unusual activity in this area. Lead researcher Dr Brown said, 'Meditation trains the brain to be more present-focused and therefore to spend less time anticipating future negative events. This may be why meditation is effective at reducing the recurrence of depression, which makes chronic pain considerably worse.'[10]

Another paradigm-shifting study (Zeidan *et al.* 2010)[11] conducted by researchers at the University of North Carolina looked at very short-term meditation practice. Remarkably, they discovered that meditation might provide greater pain relief than morphine. They found that a single hour of meditation spread out in 20-minute sessions over a three-day period produces such a potent analgesic effect on aches and pains that the researchers didn't believe their own results and repeated the process. The mindfulness meditation was found to be far more effective than simple distraction techniques.

Zeidan noted that meditation and mindfulness training teaches us that feelings and emotions are temporary. Zen emphasises developing an attitude of non-judgemental present-moment awareness. So naturally, as the practice gets established, we are less likely to focus on past or future pain.

Not surprisingly, meditation is now a popular way of dealing with pain. For example, the UK's NHS Choices website[12] lists meditation among its ten sure-fire ways to ease pain. With a

---

10 Haworth, A. (2010) 'Meditation reduces the emotional impact of pain.' News release, 2 June. Manchester: University of Manchester. Available at www.manchester.ac.uk/discover/news/article/?id=5801

11 Zeidan, F., Gordon, N.S., Merchant, J. and Goolkasian, P. (2010) 'The effects of brief mindfulness meditation training on experimentally induced pain.' *The Journal of Pain 11*, 3, 199–209.

12 See www.nhs.uk/Livewell/Pain/Pages/10painself-helptips.aspx

regular meditation and mindfulness practice you will be in a much better position to deal with the inevitable pain that arises in life.

Meditation postures

Sitting on a chair

Most people associate meditation with sitting positions. As we now know, it's perfectly possible to meditate lying down, and if your health requires that, then please just continue as we did in the previous chapters. But if you can, at this point I recommend exploring sitting meditation.

We're a culture that sits on chairs, so on a chair is a great place to start. Get used to meditating sitting on a chair and you'll find abundant opportunities to slip in some meditation in your daily life. You might want to start by reading the instructions here, then trying things out. Alternatively you might find it helpful to work with an audio commentary; you'll find one on the website associated with this book.[13]

Find an upright chair with a flat or forward tilted base. Chairs with a backward tilt to the seat put the pelvis off-line and make it difficult to sit upright, unless you can use cushions to oppose the angle.

---

13   Go to www.zenways.org/practical-zen-health.online and enter the password 'health'.

Sit down and settle the body. Ideally your hips should be a little higher than your knees and the feet separated and flat on the floor. If you can't place your feet fully on the floor, support them with a platform (a step) or cushion. On the other hand, if you are a tall person, you may find your knees higher than your hips, in which case it's helpful to sit on a cushion to give your trunk some more height. You may also find you can create a slight forward tilt in your pelvis by adjusting your cushion to create a wedge shape. The intention of these adjustments is that your seat and your feet together give you the stability of a triangular base.

Now, just for a moment, sit on your hands and feel your ischia, or sitting bones. It is through these that your upper body weight transfers downwards most efficiently. Now join your hands together in your lap, lengthen your spine and the back of your neck, and sway your body a little in all directions with the intention of settling into the balanced point where your upper body lifts out of your ischia with minimal effort.

As you arrive at the closest you can come to the place of effortless poise, allow your body to become still. Relax your shoulders. Keep your neck long and your head balanced weightlessly. Find your chin placement by imagining you have a small soft rubber ball beneath it that you're holding to your chest – your throat remains open and your chin level.

Soften your eyes and cast them downwards to the floor in front of you. You can lower your eyelids to the half-open position, or you can allow them to softly close. Some Zen teachers are very insistent that the eyes must be open. My teacher Shinzan Roshi never was. In my own experience I'd say there are certain aspects of meditation that you'll only ever explore with the eyes closed and certain aspects that you'll only ever explore with the eyes open. Over time it's helpful to experience both.

Your lips and teeth are closed with the tongue broad and resting at its most comfortable place on the roof of your mouth.

Allow your whole body to relax. Become aware of the rising and sinking of the natural breath in the lowest place within the body where you can feel it. To protect the lower back, maintain a gentle quality of muscle tone in your lower abdomen.

You are in the right place when you feel a sense of relaxation and poise. Don't worry if it takes some time to achieve this, just do your best. As long as you have a human body and mind, there will always be physical niggles. If you have any physical disabilities, just do what you can to find as much balance, ease and openness in your posture as you can.

Initially you may find you need some back support from your chair, but don't let this take you out of line and, if possible, over time, train yourself to sit upright without any support.

A few people find resting the attention on the breath leads to an increase in anxious feelings. If this should happen to you, just go back to the bodyscan practice for a little longer. If you wish you can try returning occasionally to the breath. You may find that after a certain point the anxiety is gone, or you may find that it is not, in which case you can continue with the bodyscan. Either way, you've established your foundation for sitting practice.

COUNTING THE BREATH MEDITATION

We're now going to explore a new meditation practice. You've had two weeks' experience of the bodyscan – moving your attention progressively through the body, attending to sensations. Now we're going to centre the attention on one place and keep it here. This is more challenging for many people, but has many rewards. We maintain a broad field of peripheral awareness, but with a set focus point.

Read the instructions given here. If you wish you can begin practising along with the words you read and then put the book down and carry on. Or you're very welcome to use the guided meditation audio recordings[14] or, if you wish, simply read the text first and then practise unaided.

First, reconnect with the feeling of your body in uprightness. For many people it's an ongoing process to find their truest alignment. For now, just concentrate on getting as comfortable and as upright as you can.

Allow your whole body to relax around this uprightness. As your body relaxes, your breathing also naturally relaxes.

Breathing gently through your nose (if possible), become aware of the rising and sinking of the natural breath at the lowest place in your body where you can feel it.

As you become aware of your breath, start mentally counting your breath. In-breath, one...out-breath, two. In-breath, three...out-breath, four. And so on, up to ten, when you can start again at one. Very simple. Just counting. Just breathing.

Any thoughts, feelings, memories, anything at all, can still arise, stay around and pass – but your focus point, the centre of your attention, is the breathing deep down in your body.

---

14 Go to www.zenways.org/practical-zen-health.online and enter the password 'health'.

Any time you get distracted and lose count, just come back to your breath and start again at one.

As your mind becomes more focused and concentrated, naturally you'll find your breath becomes more light and gentle. As your breath becomes more light and gentle, your body becomes more and more relaxed and comfortable.

Very simple. Just breathing, counting, relaxing.

You may find this meditation becomes more and more pleasant, more pleasurable, as you find yourself coming into a state of restful clarity. Or maybe not. Whether you have many thoughts or feelings arising, or if things are very quiet, your meditation is equally valuable.

All you do is stay with the breathing and allow life to go on, within you and around you.

It's completely normal and natural for the mind to wander away. Don't worry; simply come back to the breathing and the counting and carry straight on.

As we mentioned before, sometimes physical pain might arise. If it seems to stick around, you might want to drop your counting for a little bit and bring the centre of your attention to the centre of the pain. Just sit here, right in the middle of it, not trying to change anything, not trying to avoid anything. Notice what happens. Stay here as long as you wish and then gently come back to the breath and pick up your count.

And sometimes by this point in your meditation things can go really quite deep. So when it's time for you to finish your meditation, it's important to give yourself a little time. Gently, become aware of the edges of your body, sway your body side to side and have a good stretch if you want.

Week Three homework

Practise counting the breath meditation for 25 minutes and then for five minutes write spontaneously in your meditation diary. Don't try to edit or censor. In addition, once a day, when you're walking or going about your day, slow down just a tiny bit and count your breath in the same way you do when you're sitting. See how it feels and later record your experience.

Case study: Family doctor
Name: Lise Nys
Live: Brussels, Belgium

My perspective on physical pain has shifted thanks to meditation. A few years ago I went on a ten-day silent meditation retreat. We sat in silence from 5am until 9pm each day. It was incredibly challenging and I often felt physical discomfort in my knees and lower back. I tried to lessen the physical pain by experiencing it as impermanent. That really helped me, together with an attitude of discipline and determination to sit through it. I now realise that physical pain doesn't last, and so when I just observe it without dwelling on it or attaching thoughts or emotions to it, it becomes much easier to bear.

This awareness of how my body reacts has made me more in tune with what goes on in my head. I've made a few mini-breakthroughs. I no longer get angry with myself for losing concentration. And when, in my everyday life, I feel annoyed or sad, it takes me less time to come out of these low moods. Meditation has taught me to be a witness. When I simply stay with my breath, it gives me more inner peace.

In the past when my husband and I disagreed about something, I usually retaliated, causing a prolonged argument. Now I simply try to observe my thoughts before I speak them out loud. This lessens the drama.

My physical health has also improved thanks to Zen. I was on Ritalin medication for many years, after being diagnosed with attention deficit hyperactivity disorder. Thankfully, after learning to meditate properly, I ditched the pills and never took them again. Through sheer willpower and regular meditation, I was able to focus on completing my medical degree. Now I'm a qualified family doctor, I always recommend meditation before medication.

CHAPTER 4

Goodbye Emotional Pain

'When young I suffer, suffer, suffer; now, happy.'

– Zen master Shinzan

Settle your body into relaxed uprightness. Lower your eyes. Bring your attention to the breath. Do one round of counting in-breaths and out-breaths, one to ten. Notice how you feel, both in your body and in your mind. Now allow your eyes to lift and carry on reading.

For many of us, painful emotions have a more prominent place in life than physical pain. Guilt, lack of confidence, remorse, grief, humiliation, despair and other heavy emotions can colour our experience of life, sometimes for long periods. Some people may even become addicted to the drama of negative emotions. It's been established that we tend to ruminate about events with a strong negative colouring five times longer than we do with positive ones.[1]

---

1   Abele, A. (1985) 'Thinking about thinking: Causal, evaluative and finalistic cognitions about social situations.' *European Journal of Social Psychology* 15, 3, 315–332.

This extended rumination hints at the value of negative emotions. They typically indicate that things are not optimal and thus require some kind of response or change in direction. Positive emotions simply signal us to keep going as we are. This means that, as with physical pain, there is no way even the happiest person is going to sail through life without experiencing some emotional pain, so we all need to learn how to handle this inevitable aspect of life.

Facing emotional pain is not an easy or trivial thing. Modern Western life offers multiple alternatives to facing yourself. Zen monastery life, on the other hand, is set up to be an echo chamber. There is almost nothing to distract you from facing yourself, hour after hour, day after day. I remember when I was practising in the temple in Japan, a new monk ran away in the depths of winter. A few days later he was brought back by the police who had found him sleeping rough by a nearby river. It had been less uncomfortable for him to sleep outside in life-threatening cold than to persist and face his pain. He re-entered the temple, tried again, and did much better.

So it's very important we go gently here. The Zen secret to working with emotional pain is found in the acronym AA – awareness and acceptance. We've explored working with physical pain. When we're willing to be aware and accept emotional pain in the same way, things begin to change and heal. When we stay with our emotional pain without avoidance or judgement, extraordinary transformations happen. Let's think about how we can foster this life-changing process.

First, be aware that there can be resistance to developing a new approach to our old patterns of behaviour. Some people may even be scared to fully look. It's not uncommon to have a fear that the emotional anguish is actually endless and bottomless. In such circumstances it's hugely tempting to avoid looking. Then life becomes about avoidance. We fall into habits of suppressing our pain, rather than processing it in a healthy manner. Just because the pain isn't faced doesn't mean it's not affecting you. If you keep repeating self-destructive emotional behaviour, this will cause harm and could even ruin your life. Trying a radically new approach and facing the suffering head on takes courage and commitment, but it allows things to genuinely change.

Rather than viewing emotional pain as an enemy to be avoided or defeated, it's more beneficial to view it as a messenger trying to communicate with us and point out something about how we are living. When we manage to receive and process the message, the hurting usually disappears.

One insight that encourages us to develop a new relationship with suffering is offered by the great Zen master Obaku. He says, 'That which sees suffering is not itself suffering.' This clear and fearless eye is actually something we all possess, and over time we can become more aware of it as a factor in our lives.

Naturally, nobody desires pain, but for many people, the emotional wounds and scars they carry are far more damaging than anything physical. If we learn to skilfully approach our suffering with compassionate awareness, not only does pain begin to transform, we also develop new insights into who we really are.

I can tell you from a mountain of personal experience that the best way to be with emotional anguish is to treat it as if you were with a terrified and injured pet dog. In this situation you wouldn't just walk out and leave the dog to suffer. Nor, I suspect, would you chase it around the room, trying to catch it and fix it. Most likely, you would sit down patiently and quietly, just being present with the dog. In time, the dog would gain confidence and trust, and only then can you set about helping. When we can treat the emotion in the same way, the suffering shifts.

A major barrier to mindfulness of emotional pain is the unwillingness to be with things as they really are. It's normal to want so much for things to be different. But no amount of wishful thinking really helps. Actually, rigidity in thinking is a source of suffering in itself. What really works is to take the momentous step of being AA – aware and accepting – even of the feelings of unwillingness.

We can view this awareness as a spectrum. At the extreme negative end of the spectrum we have suppression or avoidance. Then there are greater degrees of allowing the pain into our awareness. But what about the extreme positive end?

I want to share with you a *kōan* or old Zen case. You need to know that, to this day, Japanese Zen monasteries are practically uninsulated and unheated. In the summer you're likely to be sitting in sweltering humidity surrounded by insects. In winter frostbite is not uncommon. (Shinzan Roshi, my teacher, has only half an ear on one side due to frostbite, and I've heard of monks with residual frostbite on every part of their body.) Using these conditions as an exemplar, a monk came to master Tozan and asked, 'How do we avoid this hot and cold?'

Tozan answered, 'Why not go where there is no hot and cold?'

The monk asked, 'Where is this place, where there is no hot and cold?'

Tozan replied, 'When cold, monk, be killed by cold; when hot, be killed by heat.'

What on earth does this mean? Is the teacher advocating suicide? Not at all. When you drop the separation between you and your suffering, when there is no longer any gap, something extraordinary happens – you transcend the suffering. In losing the suffering, you also lose yourself. Through becoming one with one thing, in this case, the suffering, you become one with the entire universe.

This might sound terribly mysterious, but it's not really. When you experience suffering, as much as you can, approach it with those qualities of awareness and acceptance. Do the best

Case study: Graphic designer

Name: Daniela Calderon
Lives: Dubai, United Arab Emirates

Last year was a rollercoaster year for me. I experienced some highs and lots of emotional lows. My work and my love life were causing me much anxiety and tearfulness. Initially, I tried going to the gym and doing Pilates. That temporarily released my stress but it didn't alleviate my ongoing fears. I reached a point where my life was becoming more and more troubled, and I was feeling helpless and frequently upset.

One of the things I like most about Zen is its non-judgemental approach. Once I started practising Zen meditation I realised that I was attaching many self-critical emotions to my own thoughts. In everyday life, I was also doing this to others. I'm aware of the link between my own inner critic and my feelings of sadness. During meditation I began to learn not to grow a whole tree of negative thoughts, which can lead to over-thinking and over-analysing. These days, when disappointment hits me, I am able to stop myself from wallowing in self-pity.

A year on and I'm far more comfortable in my own skin and less reliant on others for happiness. There are times where I fall off the bandwagon, but I've learned to accept the bittersweet nature of existence. And I'm able to lift myself out of low moods far faster. Today, I have a far better understanding of who I am and where I'm going.

CHAPTER 5

The Stress of Success

Roles, Time Pressures and Mindfulness of Money

'Let go or be dragged.'

– Anonymous

The pain of playing your part

We all know how stressful the negative things in life can be. But stress is bigger than that. Starting a new job, getting married, moving house, having a new addition to the family, getting promoted – surprisingly, these wonderful events are some of the most potent stressors.

In fact, simply showing up in the world, whether successfully or unsuccessfully, is a source of stress. Shakespeare famously wrote: 'All the world's a stage. And all the men and women merely players, they have their exits and their entrances.' We all appear and participate in the world. We do this through being assigned and taking on particular roles, and most of us play several of them. Society tends to foster fixed views about what is and isn't appropriate behaviour when it comes to each position. These expectations cannot possibly harmonise with the entirety of our being. We are bigger than any role. So some aspects of ourselves inevitably get buried. As a result, many of us feel constrained and out of harmony with our roles. A role then becomes a prison rather than a vehicle for expressing ourselves. And so the roles we play become sources of stress.

There can be a certain pay-off in taking the position of a victim or loser. But most of us would rather present the role of competence and success. Society rewards us for identifying with this type of persona. A successful role may provide respect, acclaim and even wealth. But there is always some level of conflict between the part of us that is suppressed and the part getting value. Typically, this starts beneath the radar of our awareness. For instance, from the outside, someone might seem to have the picture-perfect lifestyle: great relationships and well-paid job, with plenty of rewarding travel. Yet internally the price tag on this life might be half-buried feelings of inadequacy, sickness and misery.

Zen master Shinzan, my teacher, often said to me, with a smile, 'This is the only life I can lead.' Living truly and finding your authenticity is real success.

When we practise mindfulness and meditation, what we're actually doing to ourselves when we're inauthentic becomes much more obvious. It's never the role per se that's the problem; it's our relationship with it that causes the stress. If we're willing to look at the situation with full awareness and clarity, then the tension begins to melt away.

Role stress is typically a problem of identifying. The essence of the practice of mindfulness is that we dis-identify. Through allowing the thoughts, the feelings, the entire train of experience to come and go, we start to realise that we are both more and less than any particular role; the person is not the mask. When we begin a process of dis-identifying or releasing the layers of attachment, stress around a particular situation dissipates.

When people over-identify with a particular role it becomes hard to adapt when times change. For instance, Winston Churchill was a brilliant and courageous wartime leader. Through the early days of the Second World War his staunch governance kept the country from wavering in the face of the Nazis. But once the war was over he was promptly voted out of office. The people needed a different kind of leader to enter peacetime, and Churchill was unable to adapt to the new situation. His later political career could never match his wartime heights.

Many successful business, creative and entrepreneurial types become addicted to the role of being a leader in the same way Churchill did. From here it's easy to fall into the trap of becoming addicted to a title. The role becomes everything. People neglect their families and friendships and end up feeling lost, even feeling a failure despite all the trappings of success. They become victims of their own success.

Conversely, some people want to avoid taking on any role at all. However, even the invisible man or the hermit is still playing a role. It's simply impossible to play no roles at all. So how do we handle our roles gracefully?

Let me give you an example from a Zen training temple. The meditation hall leader is called the *jikijitsu* and is expected to be incredibly fierce – rather like a sergeant major in the army. He is regarded as the father of the meditation hall. There is another monk, called the *shōji*, who is incredibly gentle and unobtrusive. You'll find him quietly mending someone's sandals or sweeping the meditation hall floor. If anyone gets too upset from the strictness of the *jikijitsu*, the *shōji* is there to quietly reassure them that it's all motivated by the best intentions. Then, occasionally, usually at ten minutes' notice, they're asked to switch roles and the change is supposed to be absolutely total. In this way they both learn how to play an appropriate role 100 per cent without investing in it. We can also learn to do this.

Summing up this flexibility of approach, Shodo Yoshida, Zen master of Kenchō-ji temple and host of the Zen2.0 Global Mindfulness Forum, teaches, 'When you sit down, sit properly. If you reset yourself to zero you'll be ready to move... Instead of responding the same way each time something happens, you need to look at each case with no preconceptions and respond to it naturally. That's the realm of Zen.'[1]

So success and failure have accompanying stress levels, as does just staying in the middle. There's really no escape. When we investigate deeply enough, we can see that even identifying with being a good person is ultimately stressful. Our point of freedom is in consciously working with this stress and the pain that comes from identification and investment in our roles. We really don't need to identify with any role. Then we can gracefully and skilfully play any role. Lightness, humour and refreshment can enter into the situation.

Take a few minutes right now to list in your meditation diary your major roles in life. See if you can come up with seven or eight. Now rank them in order of stress. Which, for you, are your most stressful roles? As you focus on these, you may get more clarity on what you're actually doing to put this stress on yourself. Notice how this clarity already begins the process of changing the situation.

---

1   See http://zen20.jp/conversations/2016/part2-conversations-about-zen-and-mindfulness [in Chinese].

Time pressure

As my teacher Zen master Shinzan has aged and become more forgetful, I've started to visit a psychotherapist for guidance and supervision. He's over 70 and been in the therapy game for most of his adult life. One time we were sitting together and he commented how in his early years so many of his patients would come to him feeling bored and unfulfilled, with too much time and nothing much to do. Now, he said, the opposite is the case. So many are caught up in a frantic time-chase where they can never catch up. Even if they can meet their work commitments and the tidal wave of emails and calls, any possible spare minute is likely to be filled with social media or other digital communication, music, entertainment and (even a little) human interaction. Boredom is almost impossible.

Of course different people have always carved out different relationships to time. Back in the 1950s, cardiologists came up with the notion of type A and type B personalities. While type Bs tend to be laidback, type A personalities suffer from what doctors call 'hurry sickness' and tend to feel that life is a race. They typically try to speed up whatever it is they do and to multitask. They are impatient and may even become aggressive in the face of delays. Perhaps you're a type A person or you've spent time around one. Even if this isn't your tendency, you've probably experienced 'type A episodes' in your life.

We can contrast the rush of the type A lifestyle with periods when time drags unbearably slowly. This becomes less and less common in modern society, but people may well experience this effect in hospital or prison, for example, or when they run out of direction or a purpose in life. I once had a job where I could do three months' work in about two weeks. The dragging days and weeks of trying to look busy were an absolute torture. So scarce time and too much time are both sources of stress.

Now ask yourself this: can you remember when time was not a problem in your life? These are almost always situations when you feel 100 per cent alive and 100 per cent free. What were you doing? It might be when you were on holiday, when you were playing sport, or when you were at work. When you recall these memories, you may notice that you were fully engaged in the present moment, rather than the past or the future. The psychologist Mihaly Csikszentmihalyi calls these experiences 'flow'. All of us have experienced flow at some time in our lives. Here's how he describes flow: 'being completely involved in an activity for its own sake. The ego falls away. Time flies. Every action, movement, and thought follows inevitably from the previous one, like playing jazz. Your whole being is involved, and you're using your skills to the utmost.'[2] When you're in a state of flow, you have no time stress. This begs the question: how do you do this? Do you need to do something special to achieve flow?

Zen master Thich Nhat Hanh says not. He notes that even:

> while washing the dishes one should only be washing the dishes, which means that you should be completely aware of the fact that you are washing the dishes. At first glance that might seem a little silly: why put so much stress on a simple thing? But that's precisely the point. The fact that we are standing here and washing these bowls is a wondrous reality in itself.[3]

2   Quoted in Geirland, J. (1996) 'Go with the flow.' *Wired Magazine*, 1 September. Available at www.wired.com/1996/09/czik

3   Nhat Hanh, T. (1987) *The Miracle of Mindfulness: A Manual on Meditation.* Boston, MA: Beacon Press, pp.3–4.

Csikszentmihalyi agrees that almost any activity can promote flow. However, he found that in the ideal conditions to create a flow state, a balance is struck between the challenge of the task and the skill of the performer. If the task is too easy or too difficult, flow cannot occur. So how can we bring more of this wonderful state into our daily lives?

Some activities are just perfect for us: they're sufficiently challenging to match our skill level and, lo and behold, we slip into flow. Skiing, for example, is carefully organised into graded runs to match different people's skills. This isn't just an accident. Many people find the flow feeling that ensues is so rewarding that they are willing to put themselves to great expense and in considerable danger to achieve it. Computer games with their multiple skill levels are also very effective, although not necessarily beneficial, flow generators.

Other activities might be too easy and so we don't readily enter flow. Most people don't enter flow when washing up, but Thich Nhat Hanh can. What is the difference here? The Zen master has a trained attention. We can say that, in general, people who practise mindfulness are more able to access and stay with flow states than non-practitioners. You can imagine how much richer and more pleasurable their life experience becomes. You can do this too. I strongly advocate making it a project. Develop your moment-by-moment meditation and mindfulness practice, and focus on how pleasurable and rewarding even the simplest things can become.

When it comes to time-stress, Jon Kabat-Zinn has this advice: first, look at your expectations of what you would like to achieve in a given time. We all know that if you push yourself too hard for too long you'll get sick. Take a step back and ask yourself, 'Is it really worth it?' For each person there's a certain threshold, beyond which there is too high a price to pay.

Second, take some time every day for timelessness. In meditation we can experience very deep states that go beyond time. The flow states we can slip into an activity can be powerfully augmented by a deep, peaceful timelessness that we can begin to touch in our daily meditation. Our transcendence of time in both stillness and activity can be deeply nourishing.

Third, look at how you can simplify things. Go for quality, not quantity. Make a determined effort to look for ways in which you're filling time unnecessarily. As the saying goes, 'No one on their deathbed wishes they'd spent more time at the office.' What about you? What might you say on your deathbed about how you spent your time in this world?

Practising Zen helps us to find a strong sense of inner balance and peace. Since there's no telling how many more breaths we might have left here on this planet, it's worth learning how to live now and celebrate each moment. Then the roles we play are far more likely to align with our deepest values and purpose.

Mindfulness of money

I grew up in a Catholic family and remember as a young boy in church being electrified by the following: 'He charged them to take nothing for their journey except a staff, no bread, no bag, no money in their belts.'[4] For me, these words went deep. Here and elsewhere in the church's teachings I found an unmistakable emphasis on the virtues of poverty. But at the same time my parents perpetually agonised over money. Children kept on

---

4   Mark 6:8, from *The Revised Standard Version of the Bible: Catholic Edition*, copyright © 1965, 1966, the Division of Christian Education of the National Council of the Churches of Christ in the United States of America. Used by permission. All rights reserved.

coming, and 'We can't afford it' was a daily mantra. The tension between the ideal of being good (preferably poor) members of the church and the needs of family life was palpable. Later the strain eased, but never really resolved.

Very likely your educational experience was similar to mine. From the day I started school to the day I graduated, not a single minute of class time was devoted to even the most basic financial management. Money was a non-subject.

Later, when I decided to enter the Zen monastery, I sold my house, gave the money to charities and walked in empty-handed save for the money I had to hand over for my keep. Then, for over a decade, I had almost zero engagement with money. Looking back over this time, I feel I was avoiding rather than resolving my family's money tensions. I've written elsewhere how on a walking pilgrimage, begging my way around the Island of Shikoku, I was confronted by the priest Nagasaki Shokyo who pointed out that money is just a form of energy to be studied and managed. I'm still peeling back the layers of my own conditioning on money and realising how important it is to face this issue mindfully and responsibly.

The first version of this book contained no mention of money, and it was Jessica Kingsley, the publisher, who suggested that the title be expanded to include wealth as well as health and mindfulness. I initially resisted the idea. Then I started to realise the scale of the money problem. The 2015 survey *Stress in America*, released by the American Psychological Association, reports, 'Nearly three quarters of adults report feeling stressed about money at least some of the time and nearly one quarter say that they experience extreme stress about money.'[5]

---

5   American Psychological Association (2015) *Stress in America: Paying with Our Health*. Available at www.apa.org/news/press/releases/stress/2014/stress-report.pdf

One response to this stress is to push the reckoning forward, to go into debt. In the UK there is now £200 billion in unsecured consumer credit – the highest in history, and rising at almost 10 per cent a year.[6] This clearly can't go on.

In preparing to write this, I decided to reach out to some professionals with deep experience in the fields of money and mindfulness.

Zenways meditation and mindfulness teacher Scott Brown went straight from university to investment banking with Morgan Stanley, and spent years making money with other people's money.

'When you're a money professional, does this area of stress tend to resolve itself?' I wondered.

'Quite the opposite,' he answered. 'In the business we talk about golden handcuffs. Nobody knows what's enough. When you get more money, there's a momentary feeling of "I'm good" and it gets you addicted. The kick wears off and you're chasing for that feeling again.'

'So how did you navigate this?' I asked.

I was fortunate in that I was never initially motivated by money. That makes me a bit different from the normal run of my colleagues. I didn't leave school with the intention of making lots of money. I was just going to do what was really good fun and glamorous and I ended up making a lot of money. My first career choice was joining the marines, but that didn't work out.

---

6   See *Guardian, The* (no date) 'Business' and 'Borrowing & debt.' Available at www. theguardian.com

'So I think you're telling me that most money professionals haven't found peace with their own finances.'

Not really. For me, eventually I had to escape. Life is too short to have it run by your job. Now I'm working in the technology field and the orientation is 180 degrees different. I work to live now, not live to work. Friends that were only around me based on my money and cars and so on have dropped away. I have new friends interested, like me, in paddle-boarding and meditation. We never even talk about money. It just doesn't come up.

I asked Scott, 'From your current perspective, what would be your money advice to us non-professionals?'

These were his three top tips:

- Do what you value and what makes you come alive and the money will look after itself. Look at happiness rather than cash.
- Check in regularly with people who are not in the same financial world as you. Get a different perspective on your values and decisions.
- If you find you're questioning what you're doing too much, it's time to quit.

What I took from talking to Scott was that money is important but other things are equally important. I value that perspective. But I felt that Scott and I were coming from different directions. He knows what it is to make a lot of money and has had the clarity and courage to say 'enough is enough'. I've never made much money and actively avoided the issue for years.

I went on to speak to Lynn Exley, one of the first few women to rise to bank manager level in Barclays. After 12 years in the banking world, Lynn now teaches Zen meditation and mindfulness, particularly to golfers. Having managed a £50 million lending portfolio, and now moving in a very different world, I asked for her advice.

'Start right here,' Lynn suggested.

Mindfulness brings us into the present moment. Here you can be grateful for what you've got. Up to now, right through your life you've always had enough, otherwise you wouldn't have made it this far. Take time to feel how you most likely have more now than even kings had a couple of hundreds of years ago. Realise that 'enough' is a feeling and not any particular amount of money.

'What would be your top three principles of being mindful of money?' I wondered.

I've always been pretty cautious with money. My first tip would be to avoid risks.

Also, I've always known exactly how much money I've had. It only takes you a few minutes to check it regularly. That would be my second principle.

From inside the banking world, I've seen how many charges there are on bank accounts, overdrafts, credit cards, and on and on. But I've found it's perfectly possible to not get sucked in. I recommend you have the most simple, Zen-like banking system you possibly can. Minimise your number of credit and debit cards. Strive for clarity. Think minimalist on your finances so that you can most easily keep track of things.

I was grateful to Lynn for her emphasis on keeping things simple and clear. I next went to talk to Zen practitioner Frank Cook, of asset management firm Misland Capital. Unlike Scott and Lynn, Frank is still very much in the money game. I wanted to know where it all started for him.

'My family had a shop and bar,' Frank told me.

I started working at age six – serving customers, helping out. I was balancing the books by the time I was eight or nine. The whole money thing was wrapped up into my family's lifestyle. We were a team with everyone contributing. The customers were our friends, there wasn't any separation. Having our own business taught you self-reliance. We had our ups and downs. At one point my grandparents went bankrupt. Also an uncle went bankrupt. But we just kept going. Later I did a business degree. Now I've been looking after other people's money for over 25 years. In our company we also work as a team. Together we handle multiple billions of pounds.

I asked Frank for a snapshot of the current world of money.

I've met many rich people who are nice and kind and a few who are not. I've found it roughly the same with people who don't have much. In my experience, money itself certainly isn't evil. However, in the last ten years economic policy has had a lot to do with helping people who have money make more. There is definitely a bias. If you're already rich it's become easier to get richer. But if the gap between rich and poor gets too wide, then you have social unrest. When there's uncertainty it's more important than ever to look after your money.

And how do we do that?

'In my view, managing money is actually an exercise in mindfulness,' Frank replied.

I asked him for a plan.

If you can, pay off all your debts. Own your own property. In my own personal life, I don't do debt. In business I work with debt all the time, but you need to make sure it's ring-fenced so your personal life is protected, and then only take carefully calculated risks.

And where does it all start?

You have to keep your records, you have to balance the books. Obviously, that's where to start. Get your own house in order. I hate saying it because I know there are people out there who are really trying and it's so hard to do. But it's important to set a direction and at least make a start at paying things off. I have a very close friend who's perpetually in debt and I've seen how every part of life is infected when trying to get money to pay off this debt. It's awful; you're better off living in a hut.

Looking for further help, I found some guidance in a totally unexpected source.

I discovered that the Buddha is a source of worldly wisdom as well as liberating insight. He took a clear and unequivocal stand against poverty, pointing out that, for the poor, ethical behaviour becomes very difficult, and without the clarity of an ethical basis, inner development seizes up.

He went further. When asked about happiness by a lay student of his called Tiger-path, he laid out a sane and practical plan for mindfulness of wealth. It's very clear, and the repetitive structure just hammers home the clarity. I want to give you the plan in full:

'Four conditions lead to a householder's wellbeing and happiness in life. Which four?'

'The accomplishment of hard work, the accomplishment of vigilance, good friendship and balanced living.'

'What is the accomplishment of hard work?'

'Here, Tiger-path, however a householder earns his living – whether through farming, trading, cattle-rearing, archery, by serving a king, or by any other craft – and develops skill in that trade and is not lazy. He is clear about the correct procedures. He can perform himself and can manage others. This is called the accomplishment of hard work.'

'What is the accomplishment of vigilance?'

'Here, Tiger-path, the wealth a householder owns – obtained through effort, collected by strength of arm or by the sweat of his brow, acquired rightfully – he guards and watches it, protecting it well so that kings do not seize it, thieves do not steal it, fire does not burn it, water does not carry it away, nor do ill-intentioned heirs remove it. This is the accomplishment of vigilance.'

'What is good friendship?'

'Here, Tiger-path, wherever a householder lives, he associates, converses and discusses with householders or householders' offspring, old and young, who are highly cultured and filled with faith, virtue, generosity and wisdom. He acts in harmony with the faith of the faithful, with the virtue of the virtuous, with the generosity of the generous and with the wisdom of the wise. This is called good friendship.'

'What is balanced living?'

'Here, Tiger-path, a householder, aware of his income and expenses, is neither extravagant nor miserly but leads a balanced life, making sure that his income exceeds his expenditures, not the reverse.

'Just as a goldsmith, or apprentice, when holding up his scales can tell that by so much it dipped down, or by so much it tilted up, in the same way a householder who knows his income and expenditures leads a balanced life, neither spendthrift nor miserly, knowing that in this way his income will exceed his expenditures, not the reverse.

'If, Tiger-path, a householder with little income leads an extravagant life, there will be those who say – "This person consumes his wealth like one who over-eats fruit." If a householder with a large income leads a miserly life, there will be those who say – "This person will die like a starveling."

'This gathered wealth, Tiger-path, has four means of decrease: (i) sexual debauchery, (ii) drunkenness, (iii) gambling, (iv) friendship, fellowship and intimacy with evil-doers.

'In the case of a reservoir with four inlets and four outlets, if a person closes the inlets and opens the outlets and there is not enough rainfall, water in the reservoir will reduce and not increase. In the same way there are four means of decrease of gathered wealth – sexual debauchery, drunkenness, gambling, and friendship, fellowship and intimacy with evil-doers.

'There are four means to increase gathered wealth: (i) refraining from sexual debauchery, (ii) refraining from drunkenness, (iii) non-indulgence in gambling, (iv) friendship, fellowship and intimacy with the good.

'So, as in the case of a reservoir with four inlets and four outlets, if a person opens the inlets and closes the outlets, and there is also sufficient rainfall, in that reservoir an increase in water can be expected and no decrease. In the same way these four conditions are the means of increase of gathered wealth.

'These four conditions, Tiger-path, lead to a householder's wellbeing and happiness in life.'[7]

I've made this my roadmap in my own exploration of mindfulness of money. Let's break it down a bit.

Hard work

Obvious, perhaps, but it also feeds back to Scott's advice to do what you value and what makes you come alive. It's simply easier to work hard if you're doing something important. Sometimes this isn't possible. Sometimes we have to dig deep to find a value in what we're doing. Sometimes we have to make sure that what we're doing genuinely does contribute to overall wellbeing. There are a few jobs that don't. The Buddha clearly stated that occupations like dealing in slaves or harmful drugs are not suitable. So sit down and take some time to establish your motivation – 'I'm working hard on this because...' – using as wide or as narrow a perspective as is going to help you to give your best. Then bring your statement to mind as often as you need.

---

7   Extract from the Dighajanu Sutta, translated by myself and Meijia Ling.

Vigilance

A Zen teacher once advised me to keep a little notebook in my pocket and write in it every single expenditure through the day. This, for me, has been the beginning of the practice of vigilance of money. Nobody wants to be an obsessive miser, and that's not the point here. The point is to pay attention. For this you need, as Frank points out, a recording system. As I arrived back and started teaching in the UK, money began arriving, and although life was pretty hand-to-mouth, I still had to pay taxes. So once a year all the crumpled receipts and bank statements had to come out and be scrutinised. This was enough for the Government, but I quickly realised that it's not enough to fulfil this requirement of vigilance. So gradually I've been working on this. I don't much like money, I realised, but then I don't much like cleaning windows, but if the light's going to come through, they have to be cleaned. Make a start. Find ways to pay attention to the money situation in your life. Guard that reservoir.

Good friendship

It's so often been said – you become like those you spend time with. If those around you live in financial chaos, most likely you will too. Put some energy into finding good friends and treasure them. How do you find these good friends? The primary point is to *be* a good friend, be a giver in your friendships and relationships. Don't cut anyone off; you simply don't need to. As you shift and change in yourself, your social life will naturally transform around you. Nurture your friendships like the tender flowers they are. All will benefit.

Balanced living

This point depends on the vigilance. You're simply not going to be able to achieve any certainty about balance until you're tracking your inflows and outflows. Once you are, you can make the choices that enable you to live within your means and live well. Living in reality, rather than a financial buy-now-pay-later dreamland, will lead to happiness. That's the Buddha's promise.

I wanted to find a broader perspective, so I reached out to Zenways meditation and mindfulness teacher and sustainability and environmental activist Jo Bodimeade. 'From your perspective,' I wanted to know, 'what is true wealth?'

Pointing out the devastation caused by greedy consumption and resource depletion, Jo responded that true wealth must 'align with positive practices that reinforce a more virtuous and harmonious balance with nature – at the very least for our sustainability as a species, at the most for true happiness'.

I've been very inspired lately by the Native American practice of making decisions based on the impact on the next seven generations. Perhaps we can apply this view to choices we make around health, relationships and, of course, money.

FOLLOWING THE BREATH MEDITATION

Now we're going to work with a meditation called following the breath, for 25 minutes. As with all the meditation practices we work with on this course, you can practise sitting, standing, walking or lying down. But for the purposes of this practice right now, I suggest staying with your comfortable sitting position. As before, you can sit on a chair, you can sit cross-legged with a cushion beneath your buttocks or, if you wish, you can kneel again with a cushion beneath you or sit on a meditation bench.

Spread your knees so that you have a triangular base. This grounded triangular quality in your base can allow your upper body to, as it were, float upwards effortlessly.

Sway your body side to side, backwards and forwards like a pendulum, until you find the most comfortable upright position for you. Have your spine long, your neck long.

Cast your eyes downwards along the line of your nose. You can keep your eyes open in this position or, if you wish, you can close them. Have your hands in your lap, your body relaxing here.

Breathing through your nose, have your mouth closed, your tongue resting against the roof of your mouth. Feel the breath rising and sinking in the deepest place where it resides naturally and effortlessly.

So, previously we counted the breath to maintain and anchor the awareness. Let's maintain this for a little bit. Rest the attention on the sensation of the breath, the rising and sinking at the lowest place in the body you can feel it. Relax into this. No forcing.

As you know, there are many places you can become aware of your breathing, for example in your nostrils or in your throat, but in the Zen school we particularly become aware of your breathing in your lower body, as this helps you to remain grounded. When your body is relaxed, your breathing very naturally becomes abdominal, so relax as much as you can, allowing your body to become upright, and begin to just count the breath, to stay with the rising, the sinking, just grounding your awareness in this movement, in the counting as we know very well.

Once everything feels gathered and settled, drop the counting and simply rest your attention on the sensations, the feeling of the rising and sinking of your breath.

Very simple, your awareness is riding on the breath, anchored on the breath, but this doesn't mean you exclude anything or suppress anything; you simply don't involve yourself with anything else, so allowing thoughts, memories, feelings, sights and sounds to just arise and pass, arise and pass, and just stay with this feeling, very simple. Any time you feel yourself getting involved or carried away with thoughts or feelings, anything at all, just come back to the breath.

An eminent meditation teacher used to use the image of a busy road with a bridge. We sit underneath this bridge. All the traffic rumbling by and we just allow it to come and go, come and go, and if at any time you find you've climbed up on to the bridge and started hitchhiking off in one of the cars, then all you do is just come back under the bridge. Come back to the breath.

Maintain your awareness, your presence, making sure that your body stays as upright as you can, trying not to droop; this helps your mind to stay clear and bright. At the same time, relax as deeply as you possibly can.

As you relax, as you maintain your awareness, you may feel your breath becoming slower, you may feel your breath becoming lighter. However light, however slow it becomes, stay with the rising and sinking deep down in your body.

Any time you get distracted, just come back...ten times, a hundred times, just come back, come back, staying with the breath.

Mindful, present, aware of the breath... And in this very simple and yet very profound meditation practice there may be times when all sorts of insights about reality, about your life, all sorts of things can arise. Just allow them, too, to arise and pass. Don't focus on them, don't try to hold on to them; anything that you really need to know will stay with you after your meditation practice.

And sometimes it can happen that as you relax, as you maintain your awareness, sometimes deep levels of perhaps suffering, things from the past, grief, anger, all sorts of things can arise; just allow these things to arise and pass, arise and pass without any particular focus, without any particular worry or investment in them in any way. Your job is very simple, just stay with the breath rising and sinking in your belly.

Just breathing, allowing, aware, very simple. And do your very best to keep your body relaxed and yet upright. If you feel any discomfort in any place, do your best to release it, to relax around it. And if you feel any pain, any sense that you need to move, then just move as steadily, as slowly, as mindfully as you can. Get as comfortable as you can. Return your awareness to your breath.

Breathing, and being aware of your breathing, that's all, very simple.

And when you feel like it's time for your meditation to come to its end, then become aware of your fingers, your toes, very gently move into your fingers, into your toes, very gently begin to sway your body a little bit, side to side, like we did at the beginning of our meditation practice, that's right. Very good, and when you feel ready, begin to stretch the body, stretch the arms, the legs, the whole body, really good, stretch, that's right, and when you feel completely ready, come up into standing, ready for your next thing.

MEDITATION IN ACTION

On YouTube[8] you can find an interview I did with University of London teacher and Zen student Noriko Yamasaki, where she speaks about her schooldays in Japan. She describes how from six years old the students cleaned their school, how school featured daily *zazen* (sitting meditation) and particularly how she had a very strict teacher who taught (and pass/fail graded) mindful deportment – how to open a door in the most mindful and beautiful way, how to walk down a corridor, how to bring simple actions alive through presence and connection.

Most of us don't have a background like Noriko. But we can start bringing this in-the-moment presence into action from now. This week, take some time for meditation in action, even if it's only for a few minutes each day. You could do some slow walking meditation and continue to rest your attention on the breath.

Or you could choose another activity each day that you can practise with mindfulness. It might be something practical like tying your shoelaces, brushing your teeth, doing your make-up or doing the washing up. Or it might be something like dancing, gardening, singing or painting. It doesn't have to be very long, but make sure you do your best to engage with it with full awareness, staying in the present moment. Remember master Thich Nhat Hanh's teaching: 'While washing the dishes one should be completely aware of the fact that one is washing the dishes.'[9] Choose for yourself now an activity that you can practise mindfully like this each day.

---

8   See www.youtube.com/watch?v=gVwTUxl_Jz8

9   Nhat Hanh, T. (1987) *The Miracle of Mindfulness: A Manual on Meditation*. Boston, MA: Beacon Press, p.6.

Week Five homework

Each day practise 25 minutes sitting meditation following your breath and five minutes writing in your meditation diary. In addition, build in some walking meditation or other mindfulness activity when you can. Each day, take a few moments to note down in your meditation diary your active mindfulness experience. Also, start the process of being mindful of money. You might like to begin like I did, by building a habit of writing down every expense.

Case study: Recruitment consultant
Name: Scott Brown
Lives: Bournemouth, UK

They say be careful what you wish for. I became an investment banker in the City of London. On the surface, it was a dream job. And my friends and family only reinforced this by congratulating me on my high-flying lifestyle. However, the reality of what was happening inside me was quite different. It felt as if I was in competition with everyone. I had that ominous feeling that someone would find out that I didn't really know what I was doing. I think it's called imposter syndrome. The financial world seemed to run on fear and so I ended up creating a suit of armour to hide behind. Underneath I was insecure but I tried hard to keep up the appearance of it all being extremely exciting.

I placed a lot of expectation on myself. I was also concerned about what others thought of me. I was desperate to succeed in this so-called good career and to maintain a successful image. My stress came from not wanting to fail, not wanting to be found out. I was hugely attached to my job and scared of losing it.

When things were going well, the demons in my head were quiet or fed on feelings of pride and life felt fantastic. There were masks to this stress – I drank far too much alcohol and worked out like a lunatic because underneath it all, I didn't like myself and drove myself to perform and achieve. It was like a bottomless pit and the bar kept getting raised higher and higher, and yet I was feeling little or no real satisfaction or contentment.

When things finally spiralled out of control, I decided to turn to Zen meditation and mindfulness. Today, I feel far more content and relaxed. I have many roles including that of son, father, brother, teacher and friend. I try not to get too attached to any of them.

I'm now aware of my inner critical voice. During my meditation, I enjoy simply following my breath – it really helps me to see the wood from the trees. After regular practice, I'm able to understand what lies beneath the surface of who I really am. This has given me a deeper sense of peace. Slowly I'm realising it is about the love of being in the here and now, the journey rather than the destination.

Zen has given me an awareness, allowing me to slowly lift the curtain and see my demons for what they really are. It has begun to open what was once a very scared and closed heart. My biggest realisation was not to hide my demons as that takes incredible energy, but slowly and lovingly make friends with them. Today, I'm able to appreciate the simple moments in life. I love going paddle boarding, surfing and spending quality time with friends and my wonderful daughter Poppy.

CHAPTER 6

Taking Care of Yourself

'Looking after oneself, one looks after others. Looking after others, one looks after oneself.'

– Gautama Buddha, in the Sedaka Sutta

The Buddha says: 'Your life is the creation of your mind.' And this is true in many ways. It's easy to underestimate the effect that your state of mind has on your wellbeing. Just as some people abuse their bodies with alcohol or drugs, there are those who abuse themselves with negative thought patterns.

Conversely, some take adverse circumstances or experiences and turn them into opportunities.

The young Theodore Roosevelt was born into wealth and status but suffered in early life from debilitating asthma. At this time – in the mid-19th century – this was a life-threatening condition. Theodore was myopic, scrawny and frail, and condemned to his bed for weeks at a time. His mind, however, was strong. When he was 12 years old, his father recognised this and challenged him: 'Theodore, you have the mind but haven't got the body. I'm giving you the tools to make your body. It's going to be hard drudgery and I think you have the determination to go through with it.'

Theodore's sister, who was in the room, reports that his response was to face his father and say with determination: 'I'll make my body.'

Over the next five years, the young man worked in his father's improvised gym. He gradually aligned and strengthened his body. He took up boxing and hiking and at Harvard University became a competitive rower. He simply refused to accept the weakness in his body.

Over time he triumphed, leading an active and adventurous life, writing 35 books and serving two terms as President of the United States. In his mature years he explained his philosophy:

> I wish to preach, not the doctrine of ignoble ease, but the doctrine of the strenuous life, the life of toil and effort, of labor and strife; to preach that highest form of success which comes, not to the man who desires mere easy peace, but to the man who does not shrink from danger, from hardship, or from bitter toil, and who out of these wins the splendid ultimate triumph.[1]

There are many inspiring cases of effort and fortitude overriding challenging situations. For instance, Albert Einstein didn't speak until he was four years old. School teachers dismissed him as 'mentally slow...and adrift with foolish dreams'.[2] None of that deterred him from reorientating our understanding of the universe and winning the Nobel Prize.

---

1   Roosevelt, T. (1900) *The Strenuous Life: Essays and Addresses*. New York: Century, p.1.

2   Brian, D. (1996) *Einstein: A Life*. Chichester: Wiley, p.3.

Then there is the case of Thomas Edison. His teachers told him that he was too stupid to learn. He didn't let their negativity deter him, nor did he give up over 1000 failed attempts before finally inventing the light bulb.

There's also the example of Helen Keller, born with sight and hearing and yet, at 19 months old, she contracted an infection that left her deaf and blind. While she lost these faculties, she often spoke of the joy of life and went on to become a suffragette, an advocate for people with disabilities and a world-famous author and speaker.

In 2009, a Pakistani blogger called Malala Yousafzai wrote about life under the Taliban, speaking out directly against their threats to shut down girls' schools. While the blog gained international recognition, it also made her the target of death threats. In October 2012, a gunman shot her and two other girls as they were coming home from school. Malala survived the attack and went on to campaign for equal rights in education in Pakistan, becoming the youngest ever Nobel Peace Prize laureate.

Why is it some people give up easily when hardship hits while others go on to blossom? Essentially, some have the mental attitude, self-belief and willpower to find opportunity in adversity. They choose to focus on the positive and they don't let other people's fear-based or limiting opinions hold them back. As mentioned in Chapter 2, Shinzan Roshi often referred to a Zen-based doll, based on a great teacher called Daruma (Bodhidharma). The Daruma has a rounded and weighted base. However he is pushed, the doll always rights himself. The Japanese proverb that goes with Daruma is *Nana korobi, ya oki*: 'Seven times down; eight times up.'

As we've seen, right from the beginning of your Zen meditation and mindfulness practice, when you got distracted you brought your attention back multiple times. Through persistence your mind becomes less flighty. This persistence also develops inner resilience, allowing you to spring back up when you fall. This strength gives you a wonderful platform to build your best life. A daily Zen practice also helps you gain clarity about the things that nourish you and allow you to feel calm and centred. Conversely, you see more clearly those things and people that deplete and diminish you. Ask yourself these questions right now. In your meditation diary, write down your answers:

1. First, what three things come most immediately to mind that you can do to increase the nourishing aspects of your life?
2. What activities, things or people currently deplete your energy? Write down three ways that you can approach these activities differently to minimise this depletion.

In looking after yourself, a daily meditation practice is paramount. In addition, explore what other activities help you to remain in the present moment. I spent some time with an inspiring Japanese Zen master, Hozumi Gensho Roshi. He wrote in *Zen Heart*: 'Time, like flowing water, never comes back. The same is true for life. That is why "today" and "now" are so important. What is important is how one lives in the now.'[3]

After establishing a daily meditation period into your day, find two or three spaces in your schedule where you can fit in a three-minute mini-meditation, perhaps at the toilet at work, at the bus stop, waiting for a lift, or in the supermarket queue. Build in these little oases. They can be tremendously nourishing.

In addition to daily meditation, everyone benefits from building mindful movement into their everyday life. I like Zen

---

3   Hozumi, G. (2001) *Zen Heart*. Newburyport, MA: Red Wheel/Weiser, p.53.

yoga. It works very well for physical, energetic and emotional health. But any movement that is based in mindfulness will be beneficial.

Find other things that give you a boost. Singing lifts the spirits. As the Spanish novelist Miguel de Cervantes said, 'He who sings scares away his woes.'[4] It doesn't matter if your voice isn't pitch-perfect; the benefit is in the process. In Japan I was amazed how people were expected to have their song and would pretty much sing it at the drop of a hat. Somehow, in the UK, almost everyone I grew up around had a fixed view that they couldn't sing and that the ability to sing was rare. Japan showed me otherwise. Research has revealed that everything from humming to singing in the shower can release a cocktail of feel-good hormones. Singing also helps you breathe better – using your diaphragm – and this will reset your physiology.

Dancing is a great way of staying fit and coming into the present moment. When I lived in Japan, my Zen teacher took me to a little town north of our temple that once a year hosted a 400-year-old Buddhist dance festival in the streets. Thousands of people in brightly coloured summer kimonos dance right through the night for four nights straight. I felt a tremendous sense of joy and togetherness in those streets. The dance seemed to heal any sense of separation. Hans Bos points out how profound dancing can be: 'While I dance I cannot judge, I cannot hate, I cannot separate myself from life. I can only be joyful and whole. That is why I dance.'[5]

Notice there's nothing here about natural rhythm or ability. I recommend that you simply dance whenever and however you can.

4   de Cervantes, M. (1605/1885) *The Ingenious Gentleman: Don Quixote de la Mancha*. London: Smith, Elder & Co, p.171.

5   Bos, H. (1995) *The Crescent Moon 2*, 5, p.1.

Go for any activities that for you are generators of authentic joy. Zen master Joshu Sasaki Roshi gave the following advice:

> When you wake up tomorrow morning, first thing, stand up, put your hands on your hips, and laugh five or ten times, and that will cure you of much of your illness. This exercise is even better than a long period of meditative sitting. As a beginner in meditation, instead of suffering a long period of cramped legs, it would be better for you every morning as soon as you get up to immediately stand in this position and laugh about ten times. This is really the best beginning of Zen.[6]

If you need help getting going with this, book a session of laughter yoga, watch a comedy, do whatever makes you laugh. Animals love to laugh too. If you search on the internet you can hear recordings of rats laughing – it'll make you laugh to hear them!

If you're feeling good, activate your generators of joy and feel better; if you're feeling gloomy, do the same thing and you'll most likely lift your spirits. The trick is to discover what works for you and to simply do it.

Also, gradually infusing mindfulness into your life is tremendously rewarding. Perhaps you can start with something simple like being fully present every time you make tea. Then you can begin to spread this awareness into other activities. The road to mastery is a long one, but highly rewarding. Zen master Thich Nhat Hanh reminds us that when we are fully present, we are fully alive. He writes: 'Chopping wood is meditation.

---

6   See http://terebess.hu/zen/mesterek/Joshu-Sasaki-Roshi-About-Zazen.pdf

Carrying water is meditation. Be mindful 24 hours a day, not just during the one hour you may allot for formal meditation.'[7]

Do everything you can to be aware of the miracle of your life and the miracle of all life. Humans are social animals. Many of our greatest joys and deepest pains concern other people. In exploring mindfulness in human interactions, start with the people you spend time with. Be present when you are in their company. When you notice defensiveness and self-consciousness arising, simply be aware of it and let it dissolve. Over time you will be able to maintain your mindfulness with almost anyone. Track your progress in your meditation diary. How do you do this? It's simple really. Just each day write down your intention to be more mindful and present with a particular person. Then, later on, note down how you got on. If you repeat this process, things change. The mere act of writing will, over time, powerfully shift blocks and habits.

More than this, it's been said that we become like those we spend time with. So if you want to succeed in the fields of meditation and mindfulness, make sure you connect with friends and teachers on the same path.

It's also worth thinking about those you can help. There are many different dimensions in which you can give, and the energy of giving is tremendously positive. The Dalai Lama once noted: 'Start giving first and expect absolutely nothing.' By being selfless and giving time, support, expertise or simply your presence, you will automatically reap many benefits. It's as good for you as it is for the recipient. And as the poet Maya Angelou once noted, 'No one ever becomes poor by giving.' In fact, it's quite the opposite. Scientists have found that altruistic

---

7   Nhat Hanh, T. (1987) *The Miracle of Mindfulness: A Manual on Meditation.* Boston, MA: Beacon Press, p.24.

behaviour releases happy hormones in our brain, producing what is known as a 'helper's high'.

Another powerful quality to cultivate is forgiveness. In the context of your relationships with others and with yourself, make time, perhaps once a month or more frequently if you need, to forgive. Just think of all the people in your life you're not completely happy with (including yourself) and forgive them all. Mentally say, 'I forgive you.' Keep on saying it until you feel a shift. Stored-up grudges and resentments can become trapped in the body for years, having a negative impact, both physically and mentally. As the popular saying goes, 'Holding on to resentment is like drinking poison and expecting the other person to die.' In reality, some people in your life may well have done you wrong. They may have caused you great emotional and/or physical pain. And it's important to act skilfully and not lay yourself open to further wrongdoing. But we must still forgive. Forgiveness is not about condoning any past wrong. Rather, it sets you free and allows you to move forward. For our own sake we forgive. Nelson Mandela put it beautifully: 'Forgiveness liberates the soul, it removes fear. That's why it is such a powerful weapon.'

Also, make time for gratitude. It's a human tendency to focus on what we don't have rather than what we do. Modern culture is geared to constantly sell us new products and experiences. As a result, expectations and entitlement have soared. Along the way there's a tendency to forget to be thankful.

Research shows that gratitude is an essential ingredient for happiness. Being appreciative creates a powerful shift leading to wellbeing on a number of levels. My first Zen teacher used to say, 'Gratitude is the first sign of enlightenment.'

Each day, right after I meditate, I write down in my meditation diary three things I am grateful for. They can be big things, small things; it doesn't matter – I tend to go for what's obvious to me in the moment. The result of doing this is clear and predictable – I feel good.

FOLLOWING THE BREATH MEDITATION

Now we're going to continue refining your following the breath meditation, for 25 minutes. As this practice develops it tends to become more relaxed and more natural. As with all the meditation practices we work with on this course, you can practise sitting, standing, walking or lying down. But for now, I suggest staying with your comfortable sitting position. As before, you can sit on a chair, you can sit cross-legged supported by a cushion or, if you wish, you can kneel, again with a cushion or meditation bench beneath you.

Spread your knees to create your triangular base. Allow your upper body to come into its poised, relaxed uprightness. You're very familiar with the alignment now. Sway your body side to side, backwards and forwards, and settle into stillness.

If at all possible, breathe through your nose. You can do this meditation practice breathing through the mouth, but the nose is recommended. Become aware of your relaxed, effortless breath rising and sinking. Move your attention to the lowest place in the body where you can feel the breath movement, and rest it here.

Simply tune into the physical sensations associated with your breath, simply feel the rising, the sinking, just grounding your awareness in this movement and these associated feelings.

Very simple, your awareness rides on the breath, is anchored to the breath, but this doesn't mean you exclude or suppress any of the other experiences or processes of life. Simply allow the thoughts, memories, feelings, sights and sounds to arise and pass, arise and pass, and just stay with this breathing sensation – very simple.

Naturally at times you'll feel distracted. When you find yourself getting involved or carried away with thoughts or feelings or anything else, simply come back to the breath.

Previously we mentioned the image of sitting under a bridge. That's all you need to do, just be, beneath the bridge. The thoughts, feelings, memories, sensations can be like traffic flowing over the bridge. Now and again you get attracted by some element of the traffic and start hitchhiking; simply come back, back to the breath, back to your place beneath the bridge. You don't have to stop anything or control anything. Life goes on. You simply sit beneath the bridge and use the breath as an anchor to keep you there.

Maintain your awareness, your presence, make sure that your body stays as upright as you can, try not to droop – this helps your mind stay aware and spacious. As you stay with this uprightness, relax as deeply as you possibly can.

As you relax, as you maintain this awareness, you're likely to feel your breath lighten and soften. Don't try to make this happen. We don't manipulate the breath in any way. Nevertheless, it's quite normal for it to slow down, perhaps even to become so light it's almost like you're not breathing at all.

Simply breathing...simply aware...very simple.

Each time you get distracted, you just come back... ten times, a hundred times, just come back, come back, stay with the breath. This process is more about being than doing.

And in this being, sometimes all kinds of inspirations and insights can arise. However wonderful or profound they might be, simply treat them the same as everything else. Let them come; let them go.

Sometimes painful or unpleasant feelings or memories might come up too. Again, we treat them exactly the same as everything else. Let them come; let them go.

Your part in the process is very simple, just stay with the rising and sinking of the breath and allow everything else to come and go.

If you feel any physical discomfort in the body, do your best to release it, to relax around it. If it persists or there's any sense that you need to move, then simply move as gently, as slowly, as mindfully as you can. The body won't always be pain-free, but make it as comfortable as you can in the circumstances and turn your awareness to your breath.

Breathing, and being aware of your breathing, that's all, very simple.

And when it's time for your meditation to end, become aware of your fingers, your toes, very gently move into your fingers, into your toes, very gently begin to sway your body a little bit side to side, the same way you did at the beginning of your meditation practice. And when you're ready, spend a few minutes writing in your meditation diary.

Week Six homework

Continue your following the breath sitting meditation for 25 minutes every day and take five minutes to write in your meditation diary immediately afterwards. Don't try to edit or censor – just write out whatever's coming. Continue practising and noting your daily life mindfulness activities. In addition, each day, note down in your diary ten things you're grateful for.

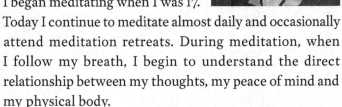

Case study: Transpersonal coach, speaker and author

Name: Cyntha Gonzalez
Lives: Dubai, United Arab Emirates

I began meditating when I was 17. Today I continue to meditate almost daily and occasionally attend meditation retreats. During meditation, when I follow my breath, I begin to understand the direct relationship between my thoughts, my peace of mind and my physical body.

I was born highly emotionally and energetically sensitive. Before I began meditating, I would often feel hurt and injured by outside forces, leading me to suffer and experience inner turmoil. I would feel victimised by certain family members, friends and work colleagues.

Meditating helped me to strengthen a non-reactive, wise stance that sees the overview and neutralises any victim perspective. It has irrevocably transformed me as a person, and has shifted my perspective on life. I now see myself as a co-creator with everything.

Practising meditation also gave me an insight and understanding of challenging forces and people in my life. It helped me give up my blame story and allowed me to see the innocence of all the players in my life. I then began giving myself that same compassion and love too. That's a wonderful place to come to.

I've also overcome several fears thanks to meditation. With regards to relationships, I held great anxiety of being hurt or hurting another. At the peak of my divorce proceedings, I had overwhelming legal challenges that woke up some of my greatest fears – losing custody of my daughter, losing residency in Dubai (I'm originally from the States) and surviving financially in a competitive city. Staying in the here and now helped to neutralise these fears and heal my blame and guilt. I am convinced that my daily commitment to meditation led us to finding an amicable win-win solution. And as we ended well, this allowed a friendly relationship to ensue beyond our divorce.

I have a beautiful daughter who often challenges me, and meditation helps me to embrace our dynamic. When my inner child takes the upper hand and my buttons are painfully pushed, I use meditation, time and time again, to reinstate rightful order in my parenting role. Being mindful brings me back to what is constant and true – the need to deeply listen to the subtle knowing, moment to moment.

Zen meditation and mindfulness have enabled me to trust myself as well as the ability to truly see the other. It has calmed my fiery, reactive nature, or at least puts me back on track quickly enough, to the best of my ability, to undo the done. It has helped heal long-embedded habits of co-dependency and keeps them in check today. Following my breath has given me greater courage and trust in risking radical honesty in all my relationships. It has opened my heart to see with compassion and love.

Bumps in the Road

Your Meditation
Survival Kit

When I first connected with Zen meditation and mindfulness practice, it was the open awareness I found most compelling. Simply being present with whatever was arising without avoidance or censorship seemed like finally coming home. It felt right. It felt honest, and then, after a while, it felt absolutely awful.

Over time I found myself emotionally raw. Memories of unhappy bits of my past floated through: schoolyard bullying, the first time my heart got broken, things I'd said to other people that were unkind and hurtful, deep feelings of inadequacy and mistrust of myself, even grief for my grandmother that I hadn't really had a chance to deal with all crashed through my consciousness in a torrent.

Over time I became more aware of the physicality of the whole process. At times, my body seemed like a mass of physical tensions. Sometimes these tensions would release to expose more buried emotion; sometimes the release would be smooth; sometimes my body would shake and quiver.

As the structure of my body and mind began to soften, there was a period where even my sense of reality became a huge question mark. Everything seemed evanescent, ungraspable. I felt hypersensitive in dealing with other people. I had a deep fear of becoming a useless person. Fortunately I had trustworthy teachers around. I was in an extremely grounded monastic environment where my days were spent in manual labour. Also, I was surrounded by fellow monks who, while not always tolerant, had a broad understanding of the process. Over time, perhaps two years or so, things cleared. While the process still continued somewhat, I found myself unburdened of huge amounts of previous 'stuff' that I hadn't even known was there. I came to think of this period as a kind of mental and physical detox. Like most detoxes, it was unpleasant. But the results made it absolutely worthwhile. I literally came alive in a way I could never have imagined. This could happen to you. And more. But I don't want you to get more than you bargained for, so I'm going to give you a kind of meditation and mindfulness survival kit.

As you're probably already realising, despite its proven health benefits, this practice has a different mode of action than simply taking a pill and feeling better. In Japan, where *bompu Zen* (practice for health and wellbeing benefits) has much more of a track record, this is well understood. But for us over in the West we're in a different situation. There's been an explosion of new meditators. For example, data from the US National Institutes of Health indicates that just between the years of 2006 and 2007 10 per cent of respondents – representing more than 20 million adult Americans – tried out meditation. These huge numbers continue to increase, not only in the US, but also in large parts of the Western world. As the survey perhaps hints, many of these new meditators have a health promotion motivation.

There is no zero-risk human activity and that, of course, includes meditation and mindfulness practice. With such vast numbers of people involved there are bound to be issues. Let's look at what these might be, what we can largely prevent, and what is inherent in the process.

First, it's possible that meditation and mindfulness practice might unbalance an otherwise stable system. There have certainly been accounts of meditators having mental breakdowns. Looking into the details, it's often that there are underlying issues that the practice uncovers. I'm reminded of a story of my father's, a keen gymnast in his school years. One of his fellow gymnasts mistimed a leap over a box, stumbled and lightly hit his head. Everything seemed okay until a couple of days later when he suddenly died. No one was to know that he'd been born with an abnormally thin skull. Similarly it's possible that a meditator may be more mentally vulnerable than anyone realises. This is a prime reason why the eight-week course asks for just 25 minutes' practice each day, no more. My own 30-odd years of experience in the field and consultation with my teachers tells me that it's extremely unlikely that anyone is going to get into trouble with this limited amount of practice. Almost always, the reported cases of imbalance involve vastly more intense practice periods.

It can also happen over time that the practice can become very peaceful and pleasurable. With certain character types this could lead to an addiction to the practice and avoidance of responsibilities in life. Again, this is likely to be rare. And again, we can protect against this misuse of the practice by limiting its duration.

Certain types of meditation that involve developing a narrow focus and excluding areas of experience can lead to dissociation – a sense of distance and separation from life. This happened to me in my early days after learning a mantra-type meditation from a Catholic priest, as discussed in Chapter 1. When I shifted from concentrative meditation to a Zen-style practice, a sense of presence and engagement re-appeared.

A very unusual (but not unknown) meditative experience is called *kuken* in Japanese, which literally translates as 'view of emptiness', but has come to mean a conviction that, because reality is ungraspable (and hence empty), it doesn't matter what you do. Goodness and kindness have no different ultimate value to evil and cruelty. I remember sitting in Sri Lanka's airport in Colombo after an intensive silent meditation retreat in the mountains, feeling that everything was profoundly meaningless. Life, death, success, failure, health, sickness – none of these things meant anything at all. There was no particular emotion around this experience, but it was very disorientating. This one-sided understanding is only likely to be touched on in sustained and deep meditative practice. Of course the ungraspability of things doesn't deny the law of moral cause and effect – the principle that different actions lead to very different outcomes. A believer in this kind of nihilism will cause suffering to themselves and others until they see the fallacy of their position. Traditionally practitioners are warned about this issue, on the assumption that prevention is much better than cure.

These problems, although potentially serious, are largely preventable with a sane and measured approach. There's still more, however – enough for *The Guardian* newspaper to announce in 2014, 'Mindfulness therapy comes at a high price for some, say experts.'[1] There is a second range of issues that is a mark of things going right rather than things going wrong. With these issues, understanding the process makes all the difference. I have heard this compared to the situation of a young

---

1   Booth, R. (2014) 'Mindfulness therapy comes at a high price for some, say experts.' *The Guardian*, 25 August. Available at www.theguardian.com/society/2014/aug/25/mental-health-meditation

woman who has never been told about pregnancy and suddenly experiences all these changes happening to her body and mind. Everything is different – how she feels, her body shape, her hormone levels, her diet. Nobody has given her any indication of what to expect, and her potentially wonderful experience becomes absolutely terrifying.

So what are these issues? They've been rather unhelpfully lumped together under the term 'The Dark Night Experience' after the poem by St John of the Cross. We've seen that the 'take your pill and feel better' image doesn't hold up in this field. Even within the field of non-spiritual cultivation there is more to meditation and mindfulness than simply stress relief and greater health and wellbeing. Added to that, a number of people, wittingly or unwittingly, use this work to stray off-piste into more 'spiritual' areas. Many practitioners, and many of the newly trained mindfulness teachers appearing these days, have no road map for what normally unfolds. But if we have a sense of what to expect and how to handle things in this process, things can unfold in the most beneficial and smooth way.

First, it's important to mention that most people are very unconscious of the amount of stress, tension and history that they are carrying around. When they come face-to-face with themselves in meditation practice, they are frequently amazed by the level of chaos in their own minds. So it can be quite a shock to realise how much stuff is floating around.

When we start to practise, what we are doing is, to use the old Zen phrase, 'turning the light around'. We are turning our attention within. We are doing our very best to relax – relaxing the mind, relaxing the body and yet, at the same time, maintaining a quality of presence and awareness. In many ways this is the magic formula for any meditation practice. On the one hand, we establish this quality of relaxation, letting go; and on the other hand, we maintain poise, balance, uprightness and awareness.

Normally, when we have, for example, physical uprightness, it combines with a measure of rigidity, tightness, even hyper-arousal. When we have experienced relaxation we tend to lose our clarity; we move closer to sleep, or at least dozing or daydreaming.

But with meditation we are bringing together relaxation of the body and mind together with presence or poise of the body and mind. When we do this, we initiate an opening process. By the very nature of things, tension, whether mental or physical, closes things down. But when we start to let go, when we start to relax, and yet maintain our presence, lo and behold, all this stuff that has been locked away within the tension and holding on starts to release and come free. The material that we close down is almost inevitably the more unpleasant bits of life, the things that we were not able to handle – the griefs that we didn't want to face, the frustration or anger around the way people treated us.

If you are willing, simply just let these feelings arise and pass while you just stay in this relaxed presence; with no pushing away or holding on, a kind of great clearing can happen. As mentioned previously, it can seem like a purging or a detox. If you ever had three days on just lemon juice or something similar, you will be very aware how during the process it is completely normal to feel ropy, even sick or feverish. But if you persist, if you let the detox work its way through, there is kind of a clearing, and afterwards you feel fantastic. Your meditation and mindfulness work contains a parallel process, but on a deeper level.

Gradually, progressively, stuff arises and releases, arises and releases. Bits of unlived life come free, and as they do, your life energy previously locked into holding this stuff down and out of awareness becomes free and available for you to use in more positive ways. Your whole being moves from tightness to release, from closure to freedom. And this feels massively rewarding. More than that, as things kind of open up on these physical and emotional-mental levels, your awareness begins to deepen and expand. You begin to know yourself more and more fully.

The big turning point, the big shift, happens when you start to see directly and know directly that the unexamined sense of yourself as a solid object or 'billiard ball rolling across the table of life' becomes absolutely laughable. It's just not how you are.

We start to see that we are a process rather than a thing. Our life is actually a dance, an ongoing, shifting, moving pattern of flow. The more we let go, the more this dance becomes vivid, alive and free. So this, often unpleasant, detox allows everything to shift from a sense of lock, tightness and closure to an open freedom.

This shift of awareness is revolutionary. Once you have seen how you really are, that you are not this lump of me-ness that is fixed and closed and needs defending against the hostile outside world, once you have seen that, you cannot unsee it again. Once you have been to Paris you can never again be somebody who has not been to Paris.

And it's perfectly possible for this shift to happen through simply persisting in your meditation and making it a daily 25-minute practice and allowing this detox process to go on. Not everyone wants this, and that's just fine. But if you have something of a sense of the territory, you can make more of an informed decision.

And there's more. The shift mentioned above is a beginning rather than an end. There are powerful forces within us that tend towards our unhappiness, towards our suffering, and they are traditionally classified as three types: the forces of greed, the forces of hatred and the forces of delusion.

The forces of greed are probably, for us in our society and culture, the most powerful ones. They are within that sphere of 'I am not good enough.' I need, I need, I need. The endless propaganda of advertising tells you that you will be all right if you have this motorboat, or this Greek holiday, or this face cream, or whatever it is. The underlying message is always the same – right now, you are not all right. And so we live in a society that is driven powerfully by this feeling of lack. In going deeper into this work, these internalised forces come into focus and, if we are willing, can be actually seen through so that you regain your freedom from what is essentially a misperception and a brainwashing.

We also contain forces that push us away from clarity about who we really are – forces of avoidance and aversion, everything from the spectrum of mild regret and grudges all the way up to full-blown fury, anger and hatred. This whole spectrum of emotions can be very powerful in a human life and can endure for years, powerfully undermining health and wellbeing.

So, should you wish to, it's possible to continue your practice in exactly the same way we've outlined. With sustained development you will see through these attraction and aversion forces, these push-pulls, and they will no longer have you enslaved. The traditional developmental road map has them reducing and then, at a certain time, they no longer drive us. What you deal with is the compulsion that the world has to be a certain way or 'I cannot be happy'. It takes some time of practice to reach this level, but human beings have done it before and no doubt will continue to do so.

There is still further to go, however. The final pinnacle of these four progressive levels deals with all our misperceptions on a more subtle level. So we become fully aligned with things as they really are rather than living in a sort of partial dreamland. As we see through these illusions they also lose their power and can no longer drive you around. So you can see this four-step process as a progressive reclaiming of your original freedom.

The thing to know is you cannot deal with any of this stuff in the abstract. You don't deal with feelings of 'I am not good enough', for example, by wishing them away. The transformation happens as they are allowed to arise in the non-reactive space of your meditation.

But in this arising, these feelings are fully here. Your job is to neither push them away nor engage with them. When we become able to do this, then there is a release. The power within the feelings is diminished.

So I'm sure you are seeing how it is quite normal in your meditation practice to feel all this stuff – these forces of anger, these old grudges, these regrets, these feelings of 'I wish I had that motorboat or that wonderful relationship or that house in the country...'; whatever it is, we let it come and go. You're simply learning how to let life go on.

This process we're involved in is simple but it is certainly not easy. But if we do actually turn the light around and face this stuff and let this releasing process unfold, freedom becomes ours. We can touch a source of happiness that nobody can give us and nobody can ever take away from us. We find our true basis and can more and more fully live from this place.

This process frequently goes on without our full understanding or full consciousness. We can come along to do a little bit of Zen meditation and mindfulness practice because we want to feel better and, surprise, surprise, this material can start to arise. If we have something of a sense of the territory, then we can see that there is really nothing to worry about, there is nothing to fight here, it is actually all fine. These things can happen and actually it is a good thing, and it is generally much better out than in with this stuff. It is mostly when we do not get it and we feel like something is going wrong or we are going wrong that the problems can arise.

In this kind of inner detox, it is important to realise that we are in charge. Most likely, if your motivation is simply a little more relaxation and stress relief, that's what you'll get. But now don't be surprised if unexpected material arises. Generally speaking, the more wholehearted we are in our practice, the more of this stuff tends to come along, but we can set the pace.

I've often said to my students that if you were going to take a donkey cart from London to Edinburgh, you would have a pretty leisurely experience and would probably be able to doze at the reins for long periods and still arrive safely. If, on the other hand, you were at the wheel of a turbo-charged sports car, you'd have a rapid journey, but a great need to pay attention and a high risk of ending up in a ditch. Most likely you'd benefit from a driving coach or something similar. With your meditation and mindfulness practice, it's similar. The more intensively you practise, the more important it is to have teachers, friends and fellow travellers around you.

It is a much better idea to do your meditation for maybe 25 minutes every single day than it is to do this in one big lump on a weekend and then nothing through the week. If you establish a daily, sustainable practice, then all of this can release a little bit at a time, and there will be minimal unpleasantness. If you want to go a little faster, then you can start to build in perhaps a second meditation session in the day. It could be morning and evening, 20–25 minutes. That works very well. If it feels like it is all getting too much and stuff is rising up that feels a bit unpleasant and you want to ease down a little, then just slow things up a little bit. Just do your one meditation period or shorten it. You can release things in such a way and at such a pace that it fits into your lifestyle most suitably. This works much better than doing what I did, for example, which was to go at it like a bull at a gate, where, for a couple of years, I hardly even knew my own name – that is not a smart way to deal with this, and gets pretty bumpy along the way. But if you have a broad sense of this process, then you can manage it. You can actually go through this in a way that suits your life and fits in with your schedule best, and you will get the best results from this detox, this unfolding. Your understanding will shift and your life will get that much better, step by step, along the way.

The great danger of laying out patterns and programmes of development is that people can unconsciously try to shape their experience to the received model. It's important to highlight that your unfolding will be uniquely yours. Think about the above as examples of what can arise rather than a fixed progression. As a final note to this little digression, I want to emphasise that this whole business is about kindness – you learning to be kind to yourself and kind to others. Make kindness your guiding principle, and you won't go far wrong.

CHAPTER 7

Elevated Function

'When you get to the top of a mountain, keep climbing.'

– Jack Kerouac[1]

Take a few moments to align and settle your body. Relax your muscles, your breathing, your mind. Now just allow your mind to be open, spacious and without any central object of focus. Simply be here. Sense how it is to be in this presence. And now carry on reading.

You'll notice how our meditation practices are becoming simpler. As things deepen, this tends to be the way. Also hopefully the gap between your formal practice and your everyday life can begin to close. I recommend exploring how you can bring this open presence into movement. Right now, lift your arm and scratch your ear. Now do it again, just a fraction slower, but bringing your full relaxed awareness to the process. Notice how much more vivid the experience can become. Where in your life are there simple activities where you can start to introduce this awareness?

---

1   Kerouac, J. (2000) *The Dharma Bums*. London: Penguin Classics Edition, p.84.

We'll explore this more later. For now, let's look into the background a little more. We already know that meditation increases stress resilience, lifts your spirits and enhances the immune system. Now let's look at ways in which meditation can boost your everyday function beyond the normal.

In Japan, there's a long tradition of people going to Zen temples to learn meditation and mindfulness to equip them for success in life. You can find people in politics, the arts, business leaders, sports, education and many other fields with this kind of background. Here's an example related by Shinzan Roshi about the Zen monastery he trained in, Shogenji.

During the 1960s, a professional baseball player called Tetsuharu Kawakami had an outstanding batting record for a winning team called the Yomiuri Giants. He was so good that the commentators called him *dageki no kamisama*, the god of batters! However, at a certain point, he completely lost his touch. He just couldn't do it any more. In this despondent state, Kawakami went to Shogenji, the so-called 'devil's dojo', the strictest Zen training monastery in Japan.

Kawakami threw himself into the Zen practice of meditation and mindfulness. Over time his game returned and he became outstanding again. Afterwards, he wrote a book about how the Zen training changed his life. Retiring from the field, he became the Giants' coach and every year he took his team to Shogenji, requiring that they joined in the meditation training. The results he got as coach were as outstanding as his results as a player.

I've mentioned before my first meditation teacher, champion golfer Father Jack Madden. Today, many sports stars – from tennis to golf and athletics to football – have credited meditation and mindfulness with taking their game to the next level. A great example is American Football team the Seattle Seahawks who, coached by meditation enthusiast Pete Carroll, powered to a 2014 Superbowl victory. To this day, the Seahawks are considered the world's best American football team. In basketball, the Chicago Bulls and then the Los Angeles Lakers reigned supreme when coached by Phil Jackson (nicknamed 'The Zen master'). When interviewed by Oprah Winfrey, Jackson described teaching his players meditation and putting them through awareness exercises like having them keep total silence for a day, practise in severely reduced light, and building mental strength in parallel with physical strength.

Zenways meditation and mindfulness teacher and keen golfer Lynn Exley was so impressed by the improvement to her playing that the practice brought her that she developed a programme to share the benefits, called the Mindful Golfer. 'I'm using golf to improve people's lives on and off the course,' she says.

There are two zones in golf. The thinking zone is where you choose your club, analyse the wind, look at the course and so on. But then you need to step into the playing zone where you stop thinking and simply be – 100 per cent present. The thing is, nobody teaches people how to make this transition. If they've practised even a little bit of technique, golfers know what they need to do to play really well. But when they're lost in thinking, effective execution becomes impossible. So at the Mindful Golfer, this shift from thinking to being is what I'm teaching them to create. In having these two zones, golf mirrors many other areas in life. When golfers can do this on the course, they can do this off the course too. If people follow my practice programme they can easily drop five shots in three months, which is a significant improvement.

In a more cerebral field, British chess champion Jonathan Rowson says, 'After meditating I feel calm, centred and ready to compete but, more importantly, the technique allows me to "just play" and enjoy the game without worrying about the result.' But not only professional competitors benefit from these practices. In my personal experience I found that after a few years of Zen meditation and mindfulness practice I had more energy to get through the day, more clarity and connection in dealing with other people, and an emotional ease that I couldn't even have dreamed of previously. Many others are finding this too.

In the political sphere, keeping calm under pressure is essential. In 2014, *The Guardian* newspaper reported that 95 UK Members of Parliament had participated in mindfulness courses.[2] That number continues to grow.

This work has had implications in business and industry. In 1929, Kōnosuke Matsushita (1894–1989), a lifelong Zen practitioner and guru of modern Japanese industrialists, set up an electronics firm now called Panasonic. In speaking of his management philosophy he liked to say, 'We produce people and we also produce electrical goods.' Matsushita wanted his 'people first' principles and Zen-inspired management methods to find an even wider arena, so in 1979 he founded the Matsushita Institute of Government and Management. His intention was to establish 'a place where the leaders of the future could create clear national and international policies, as well as the programs for their realization, to bring lasting benefit to the citizens of Japan and the world'.[3] The Institute has a rigorous four-year

---

2   *Guardian, The* (2014) 'Society', 7 May. Available at www.theguardian.com

3   For Kōnosuke Matsushita's statement, see Cossin, D. and Ong Boon, H. (2016) *Inspiring Stewardship*. New York: John Wiley & Sons, p.110.

training programme including Zen meditation and martial arts. As well as highlighting qualities such as gratitude, cooperation and the gathering of wisdom, the training particularly focuses on the *sunao* mind, the untrapped mind, free to adapt to possibility and potential. Of the more than 200 students trained so far at the Institute, nearly 70 have served as politicians.

Yahoo Japan drew attention recently by adopting mindfulness into its leadership training programme. 'Large numbers of workers believe they are listening when they aren't,' said Satoru Nakamura of Yahoo's people development department. 'Good vibration transmits, so we first want to nurture leaders who can engage in conversation.'[4]

In other fields there are many other well-known meditation practitioners. In a 2009 interview for *GQ* magazine, Clint Eastwood once said, 'Meditation with me was just a self-reliant thing. I've been doing it almost forty years. But I don't go out and sell it.'[5]

The actor/comedian Russell Brand turned to yoga and meditation to deal with addiction issues. He is now sober, living a clean lifestyle and, in his own words, 'happier than ever before'. Also well known is the case of singer and writer Leonard Cohen, who dealt with depression through practising in a Zen monastery full time for five years. Afterwards, on discovering that his manager had stolen the bulk of his assets, Cohen, by now in his 70s, calmly resumed recording and performing, making mesmerising records right up to his death.

---

4   Tai, M. (2015) 'Japanese companies helping workers quiet their minds.' *Nikkei Asian Review*, 25 October. Available at http://asia.nikkei.com/Business/Trends/Japanese-companies-helping-workers-quiet-their-minds

5   Hainey, M. (2009) 'Icon: Clint Eastwood.' *GQ*, 18 November. Available at www.gq.com/story/clint-eastwood-legend-invictus-director

Perhaps the most famous Hollywood advocate of meditation practice is actor and supporter of the Tibetan cause Richard Gere. He meditates regularly, considering that it tames his mind and encourages him to be the best version of himself. Describing his beginnings at age 24, Gere stated, 'I had a very clear feeling that I'd always been in meditation, that I'd never left meditation. That it was a much more substantial reality than what we normally take to be reality. That was very clear to me even then.'[6]

The late Apple CEO Steve Jobs was also a long-time meditator, and there's little doubt that practising Zen enhanced his performance in the cut-throat IT industry. For a time he met with Japanese Zen master Kobun Chino almost every day. 'If you just sit and observe, you will see how restless your mind is,' Jobs told his biographer, Walter Isaacson.

If you try to calm it, it only makes things worse, but over time it does calm, and when it does, there's room to hear more subtle things – that's when your intuition starts to blossom and you start to see things more clearly and be in the present more. Your mind just slows down, and you see a tremendous expanse in the moment. You see so much more than you could see before. It's a discipline; you have to practice it.[7]

---

6   McLeod, M. (2016) 'Richard Gere: My journey as a Buddhist.' *Lion's Roar*, 9 June. Available at www.lionsroar.com/richard-gere-my-journey-as-a-buddhist

7   Isaacson, W. (2011) *Steve Jobs: The Exclusive Biography*. New York: Little, Brown, p.82. See also James, G. (2015) 'How Steve Jobs trained his own brain.' Inc., 19 March. Available at www.inc.com/geoffrey-james/how-steve-jobs-trained-his-own-brain.html

Nowadays, across Silicon Valley in profit-driven companies, meditation capsules have been installed for employees.

In the sphere of the arts, one of the greatest conductors of the 20th century, Herbert von Karajan, practised Zen meditation and loved yoga. The list of well-known meditation advocates seems almost endless.

But this book is about you. In living your best life, I strongly suggest you continue to grow your daily meditation habit and at the same time put some focus on bringing meditation and mindfulness more fully into activity. A powerful way to do this is to find little spaces in your day where you can do a very short version of your practice. I remember the first Zen master I studied with being asked, 'What's the shortest feasible meditation practice?' His answer was five breaths. This comes to about 30 seconds. I'm sure even the busiest person can find 30 seconds in their day to reconnect with their practice. You may find you can make it up to ten breaths or even a bit longer without strain. The point is to find a space and build a habit of using it. Waiting in the shopping queue, waiting for the kettle to boil, standing in the washroom, wherever it is, pick out a space for your five-breath practice. Once this is a habit, find another space. Build yourself some islands of meditation and mindfulness in your day. I'm sure you'll quickly notice how nourishing they can be.

So what functions does meditation specifically improve? There has been quite a body of research of varying quality. There's definitely scope for more clarity and robustness in study design, and these practices are clearly not a panacea. Nevertheless, there are some pretty clear conclusions emerging. First, and probably most obviously, meditation and mindfulness practice improves concentration. Evidence shows that long-term meditators demonstrate higher performance in comparison to short-term meditators and non-meditators.[8] Interestingly, mindfulness meditators showed superior performance to concentrative meditators.

Elevated general psychological wellbeing among meditators has been well documented.[9] Effects correlate with length of meditation practice. Results from several studies reveal a significant increase in positive personality growth as a function of length of meditation practice.[10] On average, meditators with more experience are found to be more confident, relaxed, satisfied, conscientious and less anxious than their less experienced counterparts.

There is currently considerable interest in meditative approaches to the development of empathy. It seems that regular meditation practice causes physical changes to the brain,

---

8   See Carter, O.L., Presti, D.E., Callistemon, C., Ungerer, Y., Liu, G.B. and Pettigrew, J.D. (2005) 'Meditation alters perceptual rivalry in Tibetan Buddhist monks.' *Current Biology* 7, 15, 11, R412–413; Jha, A.P., Krompinger, J. and Baime, M.J. (2007) 'Mindfulness training modifies subsystems of attention.' *Cognitive, Affective and Behavioral Neuroscience* 7, 2, June, 109–119; Tang, Y.Y., Ma, Y., Wang, J., Fan, Y. *et al.* (2007) 'Short-term meditation training improves attention and self-regulation.' *Proceedings of the National Academy of Sciences of the United States of America 104*, 43, 23 October, 17152–17156.

9   See, for example, Brefczynski-Lewis, J.A., Lutz, A., Schaefer, H.S., Levinson, D.B. and Davidson, R.J. (2007) 'Neural correlates of attentional expertise in long-term meditation practitioners.' *Proceedings of the National Academy of Sciences, USA 104*, 11483–11488; Cahn, B.R. and Polich, J. (2009) 'Meditation (Vipassana) and the P3a event-related brain potential.' *International Journal of Psychophysiology 72*, 51–60; Chambers, R.H., Lo, B.C.Y. and Allen, N.B. (2008) 'The impact of intensive mindfulness training on attentional control, cognitive style, and affect.' *Cognitive Therapy and Research 32*, 303–322; Moore, A. and Malinowski, P. (2009) 'Meditation, mindfulness and cognitive flexibility.' *Consciousness and Cognition 18*, 1, 176–186.

10 Davidson, R.J., Kabat-Zinn, J., Schumacher, J., Rosenkranz, M. *et al.* (2003) 'Alterations in brain and immune function produced by mindfulness meditation.' *Psychosomatic Medicine 65*, 564–570; Lutz, A., Brefczynski-Lewis, J., Johnstone, T. and Davidson, R.J. (2008) 'Regulation of the neural circuitry of emotion by compassion meditation: Effects of meditative expertise.' *PLoS ONE 3*, 3, e1897.

developing larger hippocampal and frontal volumes of grey matter. These changes correlate to greater emotional stability and increasing compassion and love for others.[11]

Perhaps another appeal of meditation is its anti-ageing aspect. There is evidence that meditation practice delays brain ageing.[12] In many cases long-term regular meditators look younger than their years. Dr Robert Keith Wallace was one of the first scientists to study the effects of meditation on ageing, focusing his work on the transcendental meditation technique. Publishing his findings in the *International Journal of Neuroscience*,[13] Wallace stated that when his group measured biological age (how old a person is physiologically rather than chronologically), those practising meditation for five years were physiologically 12 years younger than their non-meditating counterparts. Even the short-term participants were physiologically five years younger. Several of the subjects in this in-depth study were found to have a biological age 27 years younger than their chronological age. This study has been replicated several times since.

Another study conducted by researchers at Harvard (and published in the *Journal of Personality and Social Psychology*[14])

---

11   Luders, E., Toga, A.W., Lepore, N. and Gaser, C. (2009) 'The underlying anatomical correlates of long-term meditation: Larger hippocampal and frontal volumes of grey matter.' *NeuroImage 45*, 3, 672–678.

12   Pagnoni, G. and Cekic, M. (2007) 'Age effects on gray matter volume and attentional performance in Zen meditation.' *Neurobiology of Aging 28*, 10, 1623–1627.

13   Wallace, R. (1982) 'The effects of the transcendental meditation and TM-sidhi program on the aging process.' *International Journal of Neuroscience 16*, 53–58.

14   Alexander, C.N., Langer, E.J., Newman, R.I., Chandler, H.M. and Davies, J.L. (1989) 'Transcendental meditation, mindfulness, and longevity: An experimental study with the elderly.' *Journal of Personality and Social Psychology 57*, 6, 950–964.

analysed elderly people who were introduced to meditation. They experienced numerous benefits and lived longer and healthier on average than patients who didn't meditate.

In an interview with CNN, Dan Buettner, author of 'The blue zones'[15] and researcher into longevity hotspots around the world, suggests small lifestyle changes can add up to ten years to most people's lives. He claims that ageing is 10 per cent genetic and 90 per cent lifestyle. Buettner states that having mechanisms to shed stress, like prayer and meditation, was of high importance in the longevity hotspots he studied and a major factor in long health and ageing.

In addition, meditators show increased levels of creativity and problem-solving abilities.[16] The calm alertness of the meditative state provides an ideal basis for dealing with life's challenges. On top of this, it's claimed that meditation can boost your IQ score – some scientists estimate IQ increases by 20 points.

Zen practice builds *hara*. What does this mean? *Hara* is the Japanese term for the belly or guts – both in the physical sense, and also in the sense of courage, grittiness and intuition. A major difference between Eastern and Western views of the human system is that, in the East, these gutsy attributes are believed to be not just inborn character traits, but also qualities capable of development. How do you do this? Through the cultivation of relaxed meditative awareness and abdominal breathing. When I lived in the temple in Japan I met people engaging in Zen meditation and mindfulness practice and developing *hara* to prepare themselves for a career in business, politics, the arts

---

15 Buettner, D. (2010) 'The blue zones: Lessons for living longer from the people who've lived the longest.' *National Geographic*.

16 Ostafin, B.D. and Kassman, K.T. (2011) 'Stepping out of history: Mindfulness improves insight problem solving.' *Consciousness and Cognition 21*, 2, 1031–1036.

or any other field that requires courage, groundedness and intuitive or non-linear thinking.

For many people, public speaking and public performance is a source of great stress. The ability to access a meditative state helps with performance anxiety. Young musicians experience high levels of performance stress and so were selected for a study evaluating the effects of yoga and meditation practice on performance anxiety.[17] Two months of yoga and meditation practice not only lowered music performance anxiety, but also reduced generalised anxiety, tension, depression and anger.

In speaking of performance, opera singer Judith Charron told me:

> Since I've been practising Zen, singing has changed for me in several ways. I always meditate before going on stage. I also do some exercises for the abdomen, what Zen calls the *hara*. I've seen how this gives you physical strength and gets you out of your head and into your body. Before I learned to meditate, my awareness during performance was tight and narrow. Now I'm aware of the choir, the orchestra, the audience, everything. Also the practice helps you to be more generous and more truthful in performance. With Zen you can treat emotions like floating clouds that go right through you. You can die on stage in a way.

A subset of performance anxiety that is gaining increasing attention is sexual dysfunction. The major cause seems to be stress. A research project looked into the application of meditation and mindfulness in this distressing situation and

---

17   Khalsa, S.B., Shorter, S.M., Cope, S., Wyshak, G. and Sklar, E. (2009) 'Yoga ameliorates performance anxiety and mood disturbance in young professional musicians.' *Applied Psychophysiology and Biofeedback 34*, 4, 279–289.

found promising results. Researchers tentatively link the good effects they saw with the ability to direct attention.[18]

Various traditional meditation texts discuss the bliss and joy arising from the practice. And the good news is that it's actually not too difficult to access some of these states, even for relatively new meditators. Experiencing a regular ongoing sense of inner pleasure is obviously highly conducive to wellbeing, self-esteem and general enjoyment of life, irrespective of your external conditions.

Ancient meditation texts are also remarkably consistent in describing powers such as the ability to read others' thoughts and the ability to foresee future events in some meditators. Perhaps the best practice advice is not to be surprised if unusual experiences sometimes seem to pop up. But don't hitch your wagon to them – they tend to come and go. I've yet to hear of a meditator who is making a fortune betting on horseracing or anything similar!

THE PRACTICE OF PRESENCE MEDITATION

Our next practice, like all the meditation methods presented here, can be done standing, sitting, walking or lying down, but for now, I suggest you adopt a comfortable seated position. You're familiar with the options – either a chair or the floor work is fine. You can read through the instructions here in a meditative state and allow the

---

18 Silverstein, R.G., Brown, A.C., Roth, H.D. and Britton, W.B. (2011) 'Effects of mindfulness training on body awareness to sexual stimuli: Implications for female sexual dysfunction.' *Psychosomatic Medicine* 73, 9, 817–825.

practice to begin, or you can follow along with the audio guidance on the dedicated website.[19]

Establish your grounded base by bringing your attention to the places where your body contacts the earth. Become aware of the triangular stability of this base. Allow your upper body to lift out of this foundation; gently sway the body side to side, forwards and backwards, letting your spine be long, letting your neck be long. Allow your body to centre and settle into a balanced, upright stillness.

Lower and soften your eyes. If you wish you can keep your eyelids just a little bit open, or if you wish you can close your eyes fully. Let your mouth be closed, let your tongue rest against the roof of your mouth so that you are breathing through your nose. Have your hands in your lap. Let your body relax.

Put your attention on your breath; tune into our very familiar meditation object of the lowest place in the body where you can feel the effortless rising and sinking. If you're feeling agitated you may even find it helpful to go back to counting the breath, but most likely you'll be fine with simple awareness of the sensations generated by the rising and sinking of the breath. When you feel ready and settled, release your attention on the breath and allow your mind to expand. This kind of practice has no one fixed object of focus. Rather, we're establishing a broad field of awareness. This practice is very simple and yet very subtle. All you need to do is simply be present with whatever is arising.

---

19   Go to www.zenways.org/practical-zen-health.online and enter the password 'health'.

In the spaciousness of your silent stillness just allow anything at all to arise, to stay, to pass and remain aware, present, in the way that a mirror is simply present. A mirror reflects everything that passes its surface without any kind of discrimination, without any kind of holding on, allowing the arising and passing.

Whatever it is that arises and passes – thoughts, memories, sights and sounds – whatever it is, we simply provide the space in which it can unfold.

The awareness, too, will come and go. Any time you find the awareness attaching on to any of the passing things or pursuing trains of thought, whatever it might be, as you notice, it immediately detaches.

Just rest in this quality of awareness, this quality of presence, as you sit here right now, your body poised, relaxed, your mind similarly poised and yet relaxed, just allow, arising, passing away, everything can be free and flowing and you just sit, very simple – aware, relaxed and present.

Any time you feel yourself getting involved in any way in these arising and passing things, then just let go, come back to the quality of awareness, the quality of presence itself – very simple.

In this very simple meditation you're providing a space, a very open space in which absolutely anything can arise and pass away; there's no censorship, no attempt to control anything at all, so just stay with this spaciousness.

Sometimes this practice can become very quiet, very still; other times it can feel like thoughts and feelings crowding one after another; don't worry. Neither situation will tell you how good your meditation is becoming. What is important is how you relate to all these arising and passing things – just allowing, without getting involved, that's the key skill that we're developing here, this light touch, neither suppressing nor getting involved, just allowing.

Your body is relaxed here, but do your very best to maintain the upright, open quality through your posture; try not to slump, try to be still and yet very balanced, very poised, so your posture itself embodies the stillness, the presence, the relaxation that this meditation practice is about.

Allow the thoughts and feelings to arise and pass away. As you do this practice, it can become more and more clear that you're not your thoughts, you're not your feelings. These things come and go.

Sometimes quite deep memories and suffering from the past can arise in this spaciousness. It's nothing to worry about; again, just allow these feelings to arise and pass, arise and pass. You don't have to do anything at all, just provide the space and the healing looks after itself.

Sometimes it can feel like you're not sure whether you're doing this meditation or not. There's so little to do in one sense. But don't worry; if you're aware, if you're relaxed, if you're allowing things to arise and pass, doing your very best to let go when you feel yourself attaching or getting involved with things, then you're doing this meditation. It's very profound. It can take sometimes a little time to become clear about the wonders of this practice, but just continue doing the simple things, and over time, some of the depths will clarify.

In providing this open spaciousness, sometimes very deep insights into who you are, into reality, relationships, all manner of things can arise. Don't try to hold on to or store away any of these things, just let them go. Anything you need to know will stay with you after your meditation period.

And when it's time to finish your practice of presence – this meditation – then very gently become aware of your fingers, your toes, start to move into your fingers, move into your toes, that's right, and very gently move your body a little bit side to side like a pendulum, and when you feel ready, allow yourself a really good deep stretch, a really good stretch, that's right, and when you feel ready, come up into standing so that you can continue with your day.

Week Seven homework

Continue your practice of presence sitting meditation for 25 minutes every day and take five minutes to write in your meditation diary immediately afterwards. Don't try to edit or censor – just write out whatever's coming. Continue practising and noting your daily life mindfulness activities. Take some time for mindful movement every day, even a few minutes. You remember how we noticed that even lifting your arm was different when done with full awareness? Find an activity where you can apply this relaxed presence, and then, if possible, a second one. Practise like this each day and note your daily life mindfulness activities. In addition, find some time every day to do a 30-second to one-minute mini-version of your meditation practice. Note the effects this has in your meditation diary.

Case study: Software engineer and taekwondo teacher

Name: Michael Pepple
Lives: London, UK

For a long time, I've been interested in human transformation. I've read many books, but I didn't have the full practical knowledge on how to bring about change and become a better person. I intensively practised the martial art taekwondo, and that gave me a sense of confidence and presence and built my decision-making skills. But I also had a lot of anger, and in certain situations it was difficult for me to be able to keep a calm mind without having to fight.

I really knew the practice of presence meditation was working for me when I noticed a shift in my relationship with my father. He often approached me with an overbearing and dominating attitude, trying to make me do what he wanted. My normal pattern was to pretend to listen, then to resist and finally verbally lash out at him. Through the meditation I gained the ability to pause and see things from his perspective to say, 'Wait a minute, he's saying this because he's suffering or because he's hurt.'

I found I could look directly into his eyes and hear him out. I could truly give him my attention while being in a place of, 'Okay, let me discover your perspective.' Even though some of the things he said were hurtful, even aggressive, while previously I would try to hurt him back, now arguments tended to fizzle out because I wasn't adding any more fuel to the fire.

The practice of presence really resonated with me because it is like the ultimate listening. You're listening to yourself and also to the outside world, and they both come together. If you're listening with a judgement, 'I don't like this, I prefer that', then you're not really seeing things from their true perspective; you're overlaying yourself.

This practice is listening in its purest form, it's a training in listening. There's not really another place in life where you get to do this, to simply listen without doing anything else. Doing this enables me to be in the world more easily. But the effects are more incredible than that. When I'm in this place of listening, things don't hurt so much; many things don't seem to hurt at all. The feeling might be the same, but it's like when something hits your back and perhaps you feel angry but then you turn round and it's just a tiny child with a ball being playful and your upset disappears. For me this meditation works in the same way. I don't take things so personally.

I think this practice of presence is for me the heart of meditation. Going forward I want to bring this listening into deeper levels of the self, those areas that initially we may not be so willing to explore. Completely accepting myself – that's my goal, being my own best friend.

CHAPTER 8

Changing Your Life

'The past has already passed – don't try to regain it. The present does not remain, don't try to hold it from moment to moment. The future has not come, don't pre-think it.'

– Zen Layman Hokoji

Lower your eyes; settle the body into upright, relaxed stillness. Just be. Take a few moments to simply be present, allowing the internal and external worlds to unfold without manipulating or controlling in any way. Stay here a while, or if you wish, bring this same simple presence to your reading.

As we've established, Zen meditation and mindfulness are good for you, and in many ways can enable you to function at a higher level than otherwise. Let's take the perspective of months and years in this work. What can you expect? First, these practices may well prolong your life and give you a better quality of life along the way, but something's going to get you in the end, and it's important to acknowledge that. Death is the ultimate letting-go process. My first Zen teacher used to say that meditation is a dummy run for death. Actually, from a certain perspective, every moment we're dying and being born.

On this birth–death journey, how will a Zen meditation and mindfulness practice influence your life?

I think a helpful analogy is to compare this work to involvement in a sport. With any sport there are various levels of engagement. Let's consider football. An occasional participant might be, for example, someone who kicks a football around with his son or friend every now and then. The amateur participant is more committed. Perhaps he's a member of a pub football team, playing every Sunday and training once or twice in the week. The professional puts the sport at the centre of his life. Diet, exercise, rest – almost everything will be focused on promoting performance. And then there is the rare extraordinarily gifted person whose dedication coupled with extraordinary natural ability can take the game to an almost superhuman level.

How does this line up with meditation and mindfulness? The occasional meditator is likely to use the practice as something to turn to during stressful times. He or she will probably get some anxiety relief for a while, but as the practice tails off, so will the effects.

Meanwhile, the regular practitioner will be building a level of stress resistance that the occasional person won't have. Heart rate and blood pressure will tend to be consistently lowered. There will be a greater connection and empathy in interpersonal relations. Plus, the relaxed awareness of the meditative state will seep over into daily life. With consistent practice, deeper insights about life will flower, giving a far more fulfilling outlook.

If you're a professional meditator – someone who typically meditates for at least a few hours every day – you're almost inevitably going to experience things outside the normal. As long as you maintain an adequate exercise programme, you're optimising your chances for a long and healthy life. States of bliss and indescribable happiness may be a daily occurrence.

The roots of suffering will eventually be cut. In addition, research is now showing that long-term meditation practice literally alters the physical structure of the brain.[1]

Then there are the champion meditators. There's a stereotype of the dedicated practitioner in the Himalayas and there is truth to the image. Tibetan meditation master Dilgo Khyentse (1910–1991) spent 13 years in caves and hermitages and intended to spend the rest of his life in solitary retreat until his teacher directed him to begin teaching. Eventually he became the head of the Nyingma school, one of the four principal branches of Tibetan Buddhism. Students described him as 'a fountain of loving kindness, wisdom, and compassion'.[2] In Japan we have the extraordinary monk Enkū (1632–1695) who, while living in caves, wrote innumerable poems and carved 120,000 Buddha statues and gave them away.[3] Even a few Westerners have shared in these rare experiences. *Cave in the Snow*[4] is an account of English nun Tenzin Palmo (b. 1943) spending 12 years meditating in a cave 13,000 feet up in the Himalayas.

I hope it's clear that each level of engagement brings particular benefits. You can step back and organise your practice at the level most suitable for your life.

In commenting on the transformative effects of meditation and mindfulness practices, some experts like to distinguish between what they call 'changes of state' and 'changes of trait'.

---

1   See, for example, Vestergaard-Poulson, P., van Beek, M., Skewes, J., Bjarkam, C.R. *et al.* (2009) 'Long-term meditation is associated with increased grey matter density in the brain stem.' *NeuroReport 20*, 2, 170–174.

2   See http://shechen.org/spiritual-development/teachers/dilgo-khyentse-rinpoche

3   See Skinner, J.D. and Hayashi, S. (2015) *In Heaven's River: Poems and Carvings of Mountain-Monk Enku*. London: Zenways Press.

4   Mackenzie, V. (2003) *Cave in the Snow: A Western Woman's Quest for Enlightenment*. New York: Bloomsbury.

Essentially, changes of state refer to the temporary effects of meditation, which can be profound and beautiful, yet impermanent. A good parallel would be the changes brought about by physical fitness that require ongoing maintenance. Changes of trait, on the other hand, refer to permanent changes that practice brings about. As you go through certain thresholds you become a different person.

The principal changes of trait that arise in meditation occur through the process of seeing more and more clearly how things really are. The image traditionally used is that of waking up – most people are asleep, caught in a dream or, indeed, a nightmare. Once you've had an episode of waking up (even a little one), you are never the same. In Zen, this is traditionally described as a change of lineage – you join a new family, the noble 'awakened' family.

By contrast, changes of state are temporary, but, when bolstered by regular practice, lead to profound, long-term benefits. This is one reason why we emphasise the importance of regular practice. The old texts state that even the Buddha, who claimed complete enlightenment, faithfully continued his daily meditation practice. There's a relevant Zen saying:

Before enlightenment, chop wood, carry water. After enlightenment, chop wood, carry water.

Now when we consider those who have made meditation an ongoing part of their life, the greater empathy that they experience typically means that there is more love in their life. The physical manifestation of love is helping others. So as your practice matures, don't be surprised if you find that your life takes on more of this flavour. Many meditation teachers consider a broadening of a student's preoccupations away from self-obsession, together with happiness in taking on responsibility for the general benefit, as evidence of success in meditation practice.

So having got a perspective on the outcomes from a life imbued with Zen meditation and mindfulness practice, let's think about putting it together. I think it's pretty obvious that you need to take a long-term view. Build a daily practice until it becomes a habit, just like brushing your teeth. Yes, you'll miss a day now and then, just like you do with your teeth, but it feels pretty yucky when you do, and after a bit it's easier to keep going than stop. Life simply flows better when you meditate.

Now, once you have your daily practice working for you, it's a great idea to build some retreat time into your year. For example, if you can take a week or a weekend once or twice a year, you'll be able to really boost your personal journey. It's very often during retreat times that you'll find the deeper insights opening up.

As I've said, it's a fundamental human characteristic that we become like the people we spend time with. So it really helps to be in contact with fellow meditators. A weekly meditation group can be an oasis, particularly in tough times. It's also a good move to have an ongoing connection with a teacher, who can help you to stay on track and move ahead rather than plateau. The faster your practice is developing, the more important this is.

It's an ongoing journey that isn't without pitfalls, but gets more rewarding the further you go. As you develop, as you face yourself, as you experience first-hand how the application of this kind attention to your suffering changes things, you'll become a useful person. You'll become a teacher. This kind attention simply externalises. Whether or not you hang out a shingle (to open an office or a business, especially in a profession), you will be able to be of help and service to others. If you want to train formally to be a teacher, Zenways has a year-long course. There are many other courses, particularly if you're a therapist and want to use this work in a therapist/client-type relationship. The door has never been more open to exploring these ancient time-tested practices and applying them in the modern world. They work. *Bompu Zen* has been with us for over a thousand years. Wishing you great success and happiness on your journey.

THE PRACTICE OF PRESENCE MEDITATION

You've had a week now exploring the practice of presence. This utterly simple practice is nevertheless tremendously profound and capable of endless development. We're going to explore it for a further week. If you wish, just read through the instructions again to remind yourself, put the book down and carry on. Or if you wish, you can follow the audio track.[5] Although this meditation can be done standing, sitting, walking or lying down, I suggest you adopt a comfortable, seated position. You're very familiar with the options now – choose a chair or a position on the floor. Take 25 minutes and do this activity slowly.

Connect with your grounding. Bring your attention to the places where your body contacts the earth. You're very familiar now with establishing the triangular stability of your base. Allow your upper body to lift out of this foundation; lengthen the back of your neck; gently sway your body like a pendulum from side to side, forwards

---

5   Go to www.zenways.org/practical-zen-health.online and enter the password 'health'.

and backwards. Allow your body to centre and settle into a balanced, upright stillness.

Lower and soften your eyes. If you wish, you can keep your eyelids just a little bit open, or you can close your eyes fully. Let your mouth be closed; let your tongue rest against the roof of your mouth so that you're breathing through your nose. Have your hands in your lap. Let your body relax.

Initially you can put your attention on your breath, but once things are settled, allow your mind to expand. This kind of meditation has no one fixed object of focus. This practice is very simple and yet very subtle. All you need to do is simply be present with whatever is arising.

In the spaciousness of your silent stillness just allow anything at all to arise, to stay, to pass, and remain aware, present, in the way that a mirror is simply present. A mirror reflects everything that passes its surface without any kind of discrimination, without any kind of holding on, allowing the arising and passing.

Whatever it is that arises and passes – thoughts, memories, sights and sounds – whatever it is, we simply provide the space in which it can unfold.

The awareness, too, will come and go. Any time you find yourself attaching on to any of the passing things, or pursuing trains of thought, simply notice. This noticing itself will allow a letting go.

Just rest in this quality of awareness, this quality of presence, as you sit here right now, your body poised, relaxed, your mind similarly poised and yet relaxed, you just allow, arising, passing away, everything can be free and flowing and you just sit, very simple – aware, relaxed and present.

Any time you feel yourself getting involved in any way in these arising and passing things, then just let go, come back to the quality of awareness, the quality of presence itself – very simple.

In this very simple meditation you're providing a space, a very open space in which absolutely anything can arise and pass away; there's no censorship, no attempt to control anything at all, so just stay with this spaciousness.

Sometimes things become very quiet, very still; other times it can feel like thoughts and feelings crowd in one after another. Simply be with what is. There's no need to judge. Neither situation tells you how good your meditation is becoming. What is important is how you relate to all these arising and passing things – just allowing, without getting involved, that's the key skill that we're developing here, this light touch, neither suppressing nor getting involved, neither holding on nor pushing away.

Your body is relaxed here, but do your very best to maintain the alignment and poise in your posture. If things start to slump, just gently return things to your balance point. Ideally your posture itself gives physical form to the stillness, the presence, the relaxation of this meditation practice.

Thoughts, feelings, memories – arising and passing away. As you do this practice, it becomes more and more obvious that you're not your thoughts, you're not your feelings. These things come and go.

There's no censorship here. We treat the trivial and the profound in the same way; we treat the present and the past in the same way. Deep and ancient suffering, or present-moment mental chitchat – just let it come and go.

This practice is more about being than it is about doing. As mentioned before, sometimes it's hard to tell whether you're actually doing this meditation or not – there's so little to do in one sense. But don't worry; if you're aware, if you're relaxed, if you're allowing things to arise and pass, do your very best to let go when you feel yourself attaching or getting involved with things, then you're doing this meditation. It's very profound. It can sometimes take a little time to become clear about the wonders of this practice, but just continue doing the simple things, and over time, some of the depths will clarify.

In providing this open spaciousness, sometimes areas of your life can clarify. Sometimes problems seem to be solved all by themselves. Don't try to hold on to or store away any of these revelations; just let them go. Anything you need to know will stay with you after your meditation period.

And when it's time to finish your practice of presence – this meditation – then very gently become aware of your fingers, your toes, start to move into your fingers, move into your toes, that's right, and very gently move your body a little bit, side to side, like a pendulum, and when you feel ready, allow yourself a really good deep stretch, a really good stretch, that's right, and when you feel ready, come up into standing so that you can continue with your day.

Week Eight homework

Continue your practice of presence sitting meditation for 25 minutes every day and take five minutes to write in your meditation diary immediately afterwards. Don't try to edit or censor – just write out whatever's coming. Continue practising and noting your daily life mindfulness activities. Take some time for mindful movement every day, even a few minutes. You remember how we noticed that even lifting your arm was different when done with full awareness? Find an activity where you can apply this relaxed presence, and then, if possible, a second one. Practise like this each day and note your daily life mindfulness activities. In addition, find some time every day to do a 30-second to one-minute mini-version of your meditation practice. Note the effects this has in your meditation diary.

How are you doing?

Once you've completed eight weeks of meditation and mindfulness practice, please feel free to complete the questionnaires on our website.[6] You'll be emailed the results and an interpretation that will give you a sense of how your sense of stress, your satisfaction with life and your mindful awareness have changed.

---

6   See www.zenways.org/practical-zen-health-survey

Case study: Marketing director and yoga teacher

Name: Susan Singer
Lives: Miami, USA

My meditation journey began when I was 25. I was keen to find a meaningful path, always knowing that there was more to life. And during my yoga classes, I realised that while I was moving my body in time with my breath, things were slowly shifting for me and I was hungry to experience more.

This desire led me to a month-long ashram-style yoga course in Arizona before moving abroad. Then, when I returned to California, yoga was suddenly mainstream and hugely fashionable. A billion-dollar industry with so many workshops and festivals happening. I started immersing myself in that world and I admit I loved living in my yoga pants, studying yogic philosophy in coffee shops and meditating all day. However, I did notice that some of the people I was mingling with seemed to spend a lot of time talking about spiritual things but not always backing up their beliefs with positive action. Soon I began to feel as if my head was in the clouds. I felt like I was living in a different world, and I lost my sense of groundedness. Ironically, I began to suffer from self-doubt too.

I found that I was so caught up in the so-called yoga scene that I struggled to grow on the other important levels in life. This frustration led me to stop meditating altogether.

Instead, I began to concentrate on my career – I was making my own documentaries interviewing creative entrepreneurs and artists about their journey to success, and at the same time, I was also craving my own success.

Then I met my husband David. He was so even-keeled and business-reality driven. He was able to pull me down from the clouds. Ironically his calm demeanour reminded me of my original purpose for meditating – to stay balanced and centred. Eventually I turned inwards again, back to my meditation cushion.

I began to meditate alone, the practice of simply being present. I began to accept my emotions and started to feel more clarity and less anxiety. For the first time I was integrating meditation with my everyday life, learning self-acceptance and learning to fully be wherever I am at that particular moment.

Today, whenever I feel as if I'm falling back into old patterns of negativity, I always meditate. I also try to meditate when things feel calm too, knowing that this personal inward journey is ongoing for the remainder of my life. Finally, I feel that I am embracing balance.

CHAPTER 9

Your First Hundred Days

So you've made it through eight weeks, that's already over halfway to your first hundred days. I recommend, if at all possible, that you keep rolling straight on and don't miss a single day. This builds you the best foundation for a sustained, life-changing practice.

Over this time, some people keep their practice at the same level. Some people find it helpful to build in a second meditation period. Some people find they actually do a bit less formal practice and put more focus on integrating the work into daily life. At different times, different priorities emerge, but I'm sure you'll agree that at all times life will be improved by more clarity, more relaxation and more groundedness, and this work will enable you to establish these qualities and more.

Over the second half of your hundred days, I suggest that you focus on making the practices yours. What do I mean? Keep the practices going, but allow your inclinations to steer what you do. Perhaps you're drawn to the wordless spaciousness of the practice of presence. Perhaps you want to connect with your body and bring a more grounded quality to your experience, so the bodyscan practice is just what you need. Perhaps you need an anchor in the midst of the swirl of thought and emotion – returning to the ever-dependable breath.

You may want to check in and change your practice day by day. You may find that for periods of time there's one practice that draws you. Either way, as long as you keep going, you'll keep gaining the results. As we saw, the research indicates there's a pretty strong correlation between the duration of your practice and the positive outcomes you can expect. Do the work and you'll get the results.

Over this hundred-day period gradually explore incorporating more of this work into your daily life. It'll happen by itself, but you can help it by making a measurable resolution in your meditation diary and then tracking what you actually accomplish. Taking an example from the previous two chapters, explore incorporating micro-meditation periods into the little pauses in your day. Track them. Write down your resolve – how many you're going to have, for example. Later on, note down how you performed.

As you establish these oases in your day, start selecting mindfulness activities. Find the simple things: the washing up, vacuuming the floor, shaving, doing the ironing. Write down your intention to make one of them a vehicle for your mindfulness development. Track how you get on. Once it's an established habit, find another mindfulness activity. Again, note down how you do. Keep expanding your range. Gradually you'll find you can expand into more intellectual and discursive activities. Again, the same formula does the trick – first make your resolution in your meditation diary, then, day by day, record what happens. Some days you'll probably completely forget what you decided to do. You'll have up days and down days, but if you frequently return to your resolution and keep on intending to apply it, you will literally transform your life.

Your daily experience will become more pleasurable, vivid and beautiful. It's down to you to train your awareness to enjoy the show.

As you continue your practice, you'll become so much more in touch with yourself. You'll also become more in touch with others. Time after time students have told me how the quality of their relationships has deepened through this work. They become able to be more fully present with others. There's less need to mentally rehearse your next clever statement.

Setting a goal of one hundred days appeals to the collector in us! It's natural to want the perfect scorecard, but of course, the question comes up – what if you miss a day? Well, it can happen. There are circumstances in which it's possible that in a 24-hour period there is not a single 30-minute space. I have two suggestions.

First, do *something*. Remember how when my first Zen teacher was asked, what is the minimum you need to meditate every day, he said three breaths? Thirty minutes might be hard to squeeze into a crazy schedule, but three breaths? I find it very hard to come up with a scenario where that can't happen.

Remembering this teaching, I approached writing this book using a similar principle – do a minimum of one sentence a day. Even in the busiest days, you can do a sentence (I'm writing this on a Chinese bus bumping towards the Great Wall). But that's not really the point. The thing is, the first sentence is the hardest. If you can do that one, you've got yourself in front of your computer, and more will almost certainly come. There have been days when I've done literally just one sentence, but they're very rare; even at the busiest times, I've found time for more. Similarly with the meditation, do the three breaths and watch it most often expand to five or ten, watch it become three minutes, five minutes, maybe even 25. People have done this stuff sitting in airports, riding in taxis, even in a public toilet or a church, not to mention sitting in the park (sometimes even in the rain). When you do this, you add the next link to your meditation chain. Not only is the time itself valuable, but you're also keeping the whole process fresh and alive in your body and mind.

I remember when I was working through a committed hundred days like this, I'd already tried a bit of meditation, dabbled and enjoyed it, and also enjoyed the results, but now things were discernibly different. The fact that I'd formally committed made the whole thing more powerful and subtly more serious. It was like my psyche was taking me more seriously and that had an effect. We're very much building a foundation here, and this foundation is something deep and valuable. In physical fitness, they've found that you need to do a certain amount of running to get the process into your body. As you do, you actually become a runner. In our field, as you put the time into your practice, you become a meditator.

Now it's really important that you hold this shift to becoming a 'meditator' lightly. Yes, you've found something that works, something that makes a real difference in your life. Of course you want to tell others, perhaps even share it. But I've found it's so important to respect the fact that other people are on their own journeys and their scenery will be different, the methods they choose to get down the road will be different to yours, and that's fine.

You can keep this stuff light by making it a bit of a joke. A psychiatrist who has studied with me told me when he visited friends he would tell them, 'I'm on a meditation kick right now. Is it okay if I disappear off into your summerhouse after lunch for half an hour?' Rather than being resentful, his friends loved it. There was some bantering and teasing, but also a respect for the process.

Frequently other people notice your shifts and changes way before you do. This is a total process; what I mean by that is that the whole of you is engaged. It's literally impossible to stand outside yourself and monitor your shifts and changes and transformations. We have some objective measures associated with this book, and also the reflective process of the meditation diary. The rest is best just left alone. Don't try to monitor too strongly what's going on. If you look after your practice, the results will look after themselves.

Treat the second half of your hundred days as your bedding-in process. Use the guided meditations as you wish – the daily process and rhythm remain the same – but now you'll typically need the guidance less and less. Gradually, perhaps even imperceptibly, your practice will become more robust.

You might have found initially that your environment was distracting outside a quite narrow range of parameters. More than that, it's normal to be surprised at how compulsive the brain is in your early days. You sit down to meditate and feel the need to check your phone or social media three times a minute. A couple of years ago, *Cosmopolitan* magazine asked me to write about FOMO (fear of missing out), an affliction in which primarily young women are haunted by a sense that the action is elsewhere, they simply can't settle where they are. You'll find this changes radically over time. The party's right here. There really is nowhere else to go. You can settle and enjoy your life wherever you are right now. There is nothing to worry about and nothing to fear.

As your practice develops it's still helpful to view it as a tender shoot. Maintain a nurturing attitude; let the roots deepen and the stem strengthen. It will stand you in good stead.

So let's have it! A hundred days. Make it your goal.

CHAPTER 10

The Rest of Your Life

How might Zen meditation and mindfulness practice change your life in the years to come?

Well, on one level, you can't precisely say. None of us can live two parallel lives, so the comparison is simply not possible. We can say you're likely to be less stressed, healthier, more empathetic, more long-lived. The longer you do it, the more far-reaching the effects are likely to be. Think of an intercontinental airliner. Half a degree difference in navigation settings over a minute or two of flying makes very little difference. But over an hour or two of flying, your location will be hundreds of miles different. And over the thousands of miles of a long-haul flight, it will literally change which country you reach.

To get the best results you need to be in this business for the long haul, so it's important to make sure you enjoy the journey. Your practice should enhance your life rather than taking it over. Every life has its ups and downs, and a matured practice will strengthen you in riding out the tougher times. But looked at over the average, your practice should bring greater life, greater enjoyment and greater kindness.

We're dealing with a tradition here. Countless years have gone into developing, maintaining and transmitting Zen practices and teachings. But we are impacted by many other traditions too. I want to pick out two of them.

First, we have the Western tradition of the scientific method. It has done extraordinary things for all of us on the planet. But it's still a belief system and has limitations. Consider, for example, Descartes' proposition 'I think therefore I am.' This is clearly problematic when we're dealing with realms where we don't think. Nevertheless, the scientific method offers us some definite benefits. We can, for example, conduct research studies on the effectiveness of these methods.

As we've seen, this research has already been extensive. One area yet to seriously open up is a comparison of the effects of different contemplative practices.

Humans tend to overvalue what they've invested in learning. Consider the world of martial arts. It used to be commonplace that teachers and students of a particular school believed their system to be the best. All this was recently tested. Starting in the mid-1990s, the Ultimate Fighting Championship pitted all-comers from different martial arts traditions against one another. Rules were minimised and early bouts were dramatic and often bloody. The process immediately highlighted the strengths and weaknesses of the different approaches, and quickly a new orthodoxy emerged: MMA or mixed martial arts, a combination of the best of the traditions. Perhaps it's now time for a new MMA – mixed meditative arts – again, drawing together the best of what human ingenuity has developed of this inner work and allowing students to make informed judgements about what to practise. This approach is not yet even in its infancy, but the potential is there.

Second, there are Western traditions of contemplative culture with potentially great benefits for health and wellbeing as well as other aspects of development. I feel very fortunate to have studied the 14th-century English language manual of contemplation, *The Cloud of Unknowing*, with Father Conrad Pepler OP, one of the 20th century's masters of the text. The great advantage of this kind of material is that there's less sense of it being a foreign import, but rather something arising out of our own soil.

In your own life, the more that this work is yours, rather than some exotic import, the better. We've already seen successful transplanting in other fields. The Indian-style cooking arising in the UK has worldwide status; Brazilian jujitsu is accepted as one of the premier martial arts in the world; acupuncture is as at home in Manhattan as it is in Beijing. The worldwide diffusion of the contemplative arts is just another manifestation of this planetary culture we now inhabit.

It's no longer weird or even unusual to be a meditator. Everyone's at it! Even the UK Government's getting interested. There's never been a better time to jump in and get going. With the understanding of neuroplasticity, we now know you're literally rewiring your brain, right up into old age. By shedding stress, you are keeping yourself younger than you would otherwise be.

This stuff won't make you 'happy ever after' – nothing will. But I can pretty confidently say it will make you happier ever after and healthier ever after and even possibly more able to transition through to the end of life with more grace and equanimity. So, in answer to the question 'Is it worth doing?', I'd say, definitely, yes.

A few things to bear in mind, though:

Progress is not linear: In this business it's not normal to find things improving at a steady, even rate. It's possible, but far more likely is a kind of step-wise effect. You can find yourself spending periods of time, sometimes considerable periods, on a plateau. That doesn't mean anything's gone wrong, not at all; it's simply how it is. Just keep going. Eventually, perhaps today, perhaps next month, the next shift will happen and you'll be on to the next level. Don't worry about where you are; focus on the process and the results will look after themselves.

You're not necessarily the best judge of how you're doing: It's not easy to step outside of yourself, so it's helpful to have a teacher, someone who is at least a few steps ahead of you down the road and can dispassionately look at what's going on and keep you inspired and motivated. More than this, the world frequently reflects things back to you. You may find people saying things like 'I wish I had your peacefulness' or 'What are you on? I want some of it.' Notice this feedback. It helps.

It's important to find ways to maintain your engagement: Even though you may not be the best judge of your progress, it's important to find ways to keep yourself motivated. Use your meditation diary to plan and track your development. Celebrate your achievements – give yourself a treat when you make it to your first hundred days, for example. Anything you can do to keep yourself going is worthwhile. Just as an amateur runner might pick a half marathon to train for, you can do the same thing. Pick an intensive meditation retreat some time into the future and train for it. You'll get lots out of the preparation and, if you've chosen well, you'll get lots out of the retreat itself.

Your personal story is just that – a story: One of the things you're almost bound to run into is a loosening up of your views of yourself and who you really are. You'll get different perspectives on your personal story and may even find that you realise that no perspective is really the true one. Your story is simply that, a story. Why is this worth mentioning? Well, as you hold the events of your life more lightly, both physically as well as mentally and emotionally, you naturally become more able to let go. Letting go here doesn't mean pushing things away; it's not about self-denial or about wishing away unfortunate or negative experiences. It simply means we open our hands to life and allow things, perspectives and experiences to come and go without resisting or grasping. As we become more able to do this, we become healthier on every level.

Your body communicates just as much as your mind: Many people enter the field of meditation and mindfulness thinking that it is purely a mental training and are surprised at how the whole business is quite physical. In this work you're training your body as much as your mind; your experience of your body and, in fact, your whole relationship to your body can shift radically over time. Sometimes the accusation is levelled that meditation can lead to dissociation or 'spacing out'. Some types of meditation could be seen to encourage this, but not the practices in this book. In fact, we could see the practices here as encouraging 'association', the precise opposite, and people who are adept at this show a quality of ease and presence in their physical reality that can be quite striking. As you tune in more fully to the physical aspect of your being, you will be connecting with a rich source of information. Your body will communicate to you what it needs. So much unresolved material becomes locked into physical tension, and through the deep relaxation achievable through regular meditation, you'll find that many sensitivities and issues will resolve. This process may take time. Frequently issues have layers like an onion. If you just allow the current layer to release and free, everything else looks after itself.

Awareness is awareness: As we develop awareness of ourselves through these simple processes, we are developing awareness, period. What do I mean by this? You will find that your sense of empathy with others will naturally strengthen. As you become able to be with yourself without judgement or avoidance, those same qualities naturally externalise. The quality of your relationships will naturally improve, but so will your ability to see where people are coming from. Sometimes, and, in fact, most often, people's motivations are good and kindly, but not absolutely always. As your personal radar develops, it will help to keep you strong and safe.

There is no substitute for your practice: You'll find it very likely that as time goes on there's a temptation to combine your meditation practice with time on the treadmill or while you're driving to work or even doing the ironing. Everyone is really busy and there's every reason to multitask, but in this case, try to avoid it. Try to keep the stillness of your meditation time sacrosanct. By all means make your activities meditative. The more mindful you are, the more alive, vivid and joyful your life can be, but there really is no replacement for the time on your meditation seat. Almost without exception the urge to multitask your practice will be motivated to generate more doing in your life. Doing is fine. Do, do, do, but maintain a little space every single day to be. It's precious – valuable beyond treasures. Many meditators are keen readers. You have this book in your hands, so maybe this applies to you. Zen author Red Pine writes, 'Practice doesn't come out of a book. Practice comes out of the mind. Zen doesn't depend on words.'[1]

Stuff always arises: Another aspect to bear in mind is that it may seem at times that there's no end to the 'stuff' that comes up. I think this is probably true and actually no cause for being disheartened. After all, you're probably not complaining that you need your shower every day. However exalted your life becomes, the laundry still needs doing. It seems as long as we have life, we have stuff. As your own stuff clears, other people's stuff rises into view. That's my sense right now. Maybe I'm wrong, but that's been my experience.

This is not a panacea: Now, an important point. The arts of mental cultivation are not a cure-all. Nothing is. Just because you exercise every day doesn't mean you'll never get sick (although it's going to promote your health in multiple ways), and we all know that. Similarly with meditation and mindfulness, you're going to get multiple benefits, but still life goes on, and issues of various kinds will continue to arise. Also, there's no substitute for a measure of balance in your life. Just because you have a flourishing meditation and mindfulness practice doesn't mean you can afford to neglect your career or your relationships or diet or any other aspect of a total lifestyle.

Allow yourself to be surprised: And finally, bear in mind that there are many fewer limitations in life than most people realise. As scientist Niels Bohr is claimed to have joked, 'Prediction

1   Porter, B. (Red Pine) (2009) *Zen Baggage: A Pilgrimage in China.* Berkeley, CA: Counterpoint, p.139.

is very difficult, especially if it's about the future.'[2] Incredible things can happen, sometimes quickly, sometimes over time. If you look after your present, you will be automatically planting the seeds of your future. May these seeds sprout and flourish in ways that foster your health, wellbeing and happiness.

2   Quoted in Ellis, A.K. (1970) *Teaching and Learning Elementary Social Studies.* Boston, MA: Allyn & Bacon, p.431.